CAREER SKILLS

For David,
the best long-term career mentor
anyone could hope to have;
and Sue too,
who assists every day

Career Skills

A Guide to Long-term Success

Patrick Forsyth

CASSELL

Cassell

Wellington House
125 Strand
London WC2R 0BB

370 Lexington Avenue
New York
NY 10017-6550

www.cassell.co.uk

First published 1998.

British Library Cataloguing-in-Publication Data
A catalogue record for this book is available from the British Library.

ISBN 0–304–70417–2

Typeset by Kenneth Burnley, Wirral, Cheshire.
Printed and bound in Great Britain by Biddles Ltd, Guildford and King's Lynn.

Contents

0025000

Preface:
Springboard to Success

'Life is what happens while you are making other plans.'

THE ABOVE WORDS encapsulate a painful thought. All too often, we are conscious of things happening to us. If they are good things, we are apt to take them in our stride, putting them down either to our underlying brilliance, or to 'good luck'. However, if they are not so good, we blame 'bad luck' rather than our own lack of foresight. In the latter case certain things are, with hindsight, clearly predictable and may lead swiftly to our sighing 'If only . . . ' Similarly, good things that occur may also represent lost opportunities; they are good but could have been better. If we are ready for them or if we are quick enough on our feet, then we can take more advantage of them.

At the same time, there are some things that we plan, like going away on holiday; and others which we may not see as plannable, as we do not try to control tomorrow's weather. Your career should surely be among those important aspects of your life which you will want to influence. It is also something you cannot realistically direct exactly as you want. But that is no reason for not taking any action possible to steer it in the direction that you want. You must not let perfection be the enemy of the good. In other words, just because you will not be Chief Executive tomorrow if you snap your fingers and shout 'Promotion!', is no reason for not working at those factors that can take you in the right direction. And, as we shall see, there are many such factors.

Making and creating progress

This book is not about the initial process of obtaining a job (though certain elements involved in so doing crop up along the way); it is about planning where you want to go and taking action, both in the way you work in your current job and by other means, to ensure you make progress. Such progress may be measured in terms of position, of rewards (financial and otherwise), recognition, responsibility and authority. Everyone will see this in their own way. For some, the trappings of office are more important than to others. For others, money is the only measure. However you measure it, your ability to achieve what you want is not, in the real world, only a question of competence. There are organizations the world over with many people working in them who could do well in a more senior position; there are also some who are in senior positions and not carrying out their responsibilities very well, and many more who will never rise above a certain level for all their good work.

While most people would claim a degree of ambition, what is it that differentiates between those who do well and move up an organization, who hold management positions and move on to the senior levels, and others who do less well? Competence is clearly one factor, but there are others. Some of the additional factors are concerned with skills, some with perceptions – how people are seen. Whatever they are, they create a total picture that combines to influence the likelihood of an individual making progress. It is these factors that this book reviews. It does not offer a magic formula. If there was a magic way to ensure that you became rich, famous, irresistible to the opposite sex and Chief Executive overnight, you would not find it in a book at this price! But you *can* increase the chances of success, and you may be able to increase them significantly.

Before going any further it is important to put matters in a topical context.

The new realities

It is a truism to say that we live in dynamic times. In the world of business this is certainly the case. Not all recent changes have been positive, and in the last few years the press has been full of words that reflect the negative side of business change: recession, downsizing, redundancy, cut-back, closure, stress, glass ceiling, short-term contract, and more.

Some of what has occurred easily prompts regret or resentment. It may well be that there are things about the 'good old days' in terms of employment that were or seemed better. 'A job for life' is not a phrase one hears much of at the dawn of the new millennium.

But there is all the difference in the world between regretting or resenting something and doing something about it. We may not be able to turn the clock back, but we can take a practical view of the new realities.

The fact that employment now includes new options and that you may get involved in portfolio careers, home or tele-working, or short-term contracts (of which more later) does not mean that you should not work at securing and developing your current position. Nor does it mean that you should not be thinking about making its potential successor more likely to be what you want. Both can be influenced positively by how you plan, and by the attitude you strike and the action you take. It is primarily this ongoing process of career planning that we are concerned with here.

The intended reader

This book is for those who want to enjoy a successful career in business. More particularly, it is for those who wish to influence their careers towards success. You may be in the early stages of your career, or in mid-career (it is never too late to take a constructive view of what you are doing and where you are going), or you may still be completing your education and getting ready to embark on a business career. As progress in business tends to be equated with management, the term 'manager' is used in the text, though the functional area of the business involved is not specific. You may be in general management, in sales, marketing, finance, production or in some specialist area such as computers, personnel or research.

The emphasis throughout is on those things that have a bearing on what you do, how others will react to what you do and thus which are likely to have a bearing on your success. Some of these are specific to career development. Others suggest you use skills, techniques or activities which you will, or could be, using to serve career development purposes in addition to their normal role. It is not the intention – indeed, it could not be in a short book – to explain every aspect of the general business techniques involved. However, it will help you identify those things you need to become involved with, seek out more information about or training in, and those which, unless you appreciate their career implications, you might otherwise neglect. Whatever field of business you are in and however high within it you intend to rise, you will find ideas here which will help you build a career more certainly than if the process is left to chance.

The way forward

Progress cannot be made without thought and effort. Both are nearly always necessary if anything worthwhile is to be achieved. But the very fact that many different factors are involved increases the possibilities of your being able to swing the odds more in your favour. Everyone is likely to do better, and progress more certainly, if they think about it. Of the many things that are referred to in this book some can give *you* an opportunity to make a difference.

What is more, the development of a career is essentially a competitive process. Most organizations have a pyramid-shaped structure and, as the old saying has it: 'There are more Indians than Chiefs.' You need to appreciate the most basic factors, these are things which anyone prepared to spend a little time and effort can achieve, because if you lag in these areas you allow potential advantage to go by default. You also need to find other things which your abilities and outlook allow you to excel in, so that overall you are able to create the right climate for progress.

Career development is not simply an option, nor is being ambitious sufficient to guarantee success. In today's competitive commercial environment, active career development is essential. Doing nothing towards deciding where you are going and how you will get there, not even thinking it through, is a sure recipe for missing opportunities and doing less well than may be possible. This book aims to help you to think career development through in the right way, and to give you some specific ideas and advice as to what works best.

Thereafter it is up to you. In every sense, the greatest asset you have in developing your own career is simply – yourself.

Patrick Forsyth
Touchstone Training & Consultancy
28 Salcote Maltings, Heybridge, Essex CM9 4QP
June 1998

Acknowledgements

LIKE MANY PEOPLE, no doubt, my own career has not gone entirely the way I originally intended. I started my working life with a major publishing company and thought I wanted to be an editor (writing books keeps me in touch with this fascinating profession and is, I sometimes think, a kind of revenge for not moving as successfully up the publishing ladder as I originally wanted to do). Since then it has progressed, influenced both by luck and by my consciously taking advantage of luck or circumstances, and – I like to think – by the efforts I have put into my own career development. I may not rule the world, but I now run my own business, contrive to make a reasonable living and enjoy very much the majority of the things I do and, what is more, always have done. And I still have ambitions and would not wish them to run out. So it could have been very much worse. Does this qualify me to write about career development?

Thinking about this since completing the manuscript for this book, I should perhaps say something about where these thoughts originated from. They come, almost exclusively, from observation. This includes observation of what has occurred and worked well – or not – in my own career, and what I have seen around me in the various groups of people with whom I have worked in large and small organizations, particularly those I have worked with as a consultant and trainer.

So thanks are due to all those who have actively helped my career, to some who have unwittingly helped it – and also to a few who have done the reverse! I have learnt from them all. Looking back, I believe I could have learnt more that would have helped my career sooner than I in fact did, but we all have 20/20 hindsight (and I did not have this book to guide me!). Anyway, I hope this book may prompt you to develop an active approach to managing your own career, and do so in time to make a difference.

It is an area where every positive influence is to be welcomed.

For all of us there is so much to be learnt from others. It has been my good fortune to be able to rub shoulders with certain people from whom what could be learnt was useful, and with some who gave of their assistance and advice so freely.

1 / First Principles

'Winners never quit and quitters never win.'
Vince Lombardi

DICTIONARIES define the word 'careerist' as a person intent on advancement in a career. But being intent on something is not the same as doing something about it. Career development has much in common with many aspects of management. If it is to make a difference then it must start with clear objectives, and the developer must adopt the right attitude towards it and cultivate the willingness to see a plan through to fruition. The process is not all-consuming and there is no need to be obsessive about it, but it is, as we will see, something that can be worked at regularly while in a job, and opportunities to influence progress appear in many guises. In this first chapter we start by reviewing some of the overall, yet disparate, issues that must be addressed as a prerequisite of successful career development.

Adopt the right overall approach

In the Preface, the point was made that there is no magic formula which can guarantee that you enjoy a successful career. Here we discuss what may seem a general point, yet it is probably as close to such a magic formula as exists. Career development is an *active* process: you have to work at it. That is not to say that you have to do nothing else. In fact much of what needs to be done is an integral part of the work you will be doing, only needing a career development focus putting on it as well.

Any career is influenced by a thousand and one different factors. The organization you work for, the people you work with and for, and the differing circumstances of each, all affect how you will progress. You cannot possibly predict everything that will occur along the way. What you *can* do is have a clear idea of the things that will help you as time goes by, so that you can keep a hand on the tiller, as it were. Being prepared to work at it is the first step (you see the need or you would probably not have purchased this book), but you cannot just work at it in a vacuum. Some analysis of you, your situation and prospects are helpful. Also useful, perhaps essential, is a plan: something that can be drawn from the analysis. Both are investigated in a moment. So, the starting point is an appreciation of the necessity for career development, a resolve to work at it systematically – attitudes that becomes habits – and then an ongoing study of how you can make a difference, and the application of any individual methods that you judge to suit your circumstances.

For the most part, the people you hope to emulate have not reached their positions by good fortune. Of course, good luck may have had something to do with it, but it is not something you should ever rely upon – just sitting back and hoping for a lucky break is *not* career planning – and, if and when it does arrive, it needs to be taken advantage of, developed and its impact made permanent. The only element that you can guarantee will always be there to assist you, is you. So think of yourself as an active careerist and go on from there.

Decide what qualifications you need

It is said that you cannot have too many qualifications. To an extent this is true, though there are those who become perpetual students and never seem in danger of escaping into the real world at all. Here the first thing to consider is something about getting the balance right. First, let us put on one side basic school examinations. These are clearly important and some are necessary as mandatory conditions to enter the next stage (in the way that a university course in some science subject may be dependent on a candidate passing A-level mathematics).

We will also bypass those qualifications which are mandatory for particular fields of activity; for example if you wish to be an accountant, you have to pass the necessary exams. There is no decision to make here. If you want to get into a particular field, you must study and pass the relevant qualification.

On the other hand, many qualifications are much less specific. How do you know, in advance, what an MBA will do for you, for instance? Such qualifications can be useful. They may not, however, from an employer's point of view, be any guarantee of automatic competence; in my own field of marketing, there are certainly people with paper qualifications in the subject who have no marketing flair whatsoever. Such degrees do, of course, give some signs, namely:

- They impart a great deal of knowledge.
- They improve thinking abilities (developing approaches to, for example, problem-solving).
- They develop skills, though they are often less effective at this than at gathering knowledge (certain courses blend different elements very well, for example, as with many programmes nowadays that combine a management degree with language study).
- They give you a 'label', and demonstrate commitment.

It is this last point that needs some thought. Different qualifications are seen in different lights. This applies to both the qualification and to the institution from which it comes. There is a compromise to be made here for those at the stage of seeking qualifications. Where will you be accepted? Where geographically do you want to be? How long is the course? What are the financial considerations? This kind of consideration is even more difficult if you are contemplating a post-graduate qualification, perhaps one that needs a break from work or private funding. When employers talk about what they want from their employees, they tend to link closely together 'qualifications and experience' – this is what goes on a CV also – and the two do go together. In other words, while you are studying you do not get any work experience, and vice versa. Part-time courses do exist to mix the two factors, but you may find the perception of them is also different from their full-time equivalents (with solitary study not regarded in the same way as life on campus).

So another balance that must be struck is between what advantage you will gain from, say, a year working, and the same year spent on something more academic. Remember too that qualifications are used as a screen in recruitment. An employer who puts 'must be a graduate' in the text of an advertisement may be reflecting a special requirement (an engineering qualification, for example, may be a practical necessity) or just trying to reduce the overall number who apply, and obtain a manageable number of people who represent a base level of candidate.

One more point: there is also a fashion element in how some of these things are regarded, with one institution seeming to be in favour at one moment, then another. All in all, you need to think long and hard about what will suit you best, what will give you the greatest career advantage in terms of both what you will learn and how the qualification will be seen, and then make a decision, remembering both the saying that 'you cannot have too many qualifications' and the various practicalities.

Insist on a job description

Lack of a job description makes it difficult to assess a job at interview, and difficult to function in a job once you have it. This seems obvious and important, yet curiously I so often come across people and organizations where the whole area of job definition (and appraisal, which is touched on later) is ill-defined or non-existent.

First, it is important from the point of view of any organization. If managers are to manage, and manage effectively, then the organization structure, and who does what, must be thought through, agreed and documented, and the whole process must link with the corporate objectives centrally and at the level of individual divisions or departments. What is more, whatever the formal benefits of a system of job definition, evaluation and appraisal (and they are undoubtedly a vital tool for personnel and other considerations) they are – or should be – working documents. In other words, they should act as a guide to individual managers and staff in day-to-day operational terms. You will gather that I am in favour of job descriptions.

But consider it also from the individual's point of view. Surely everybody wants to know whether they are doing a good job or not – a sense of achievement is, after all, a basic human motivation coming from any work. How can you possibly gauge if you are being successful if the job in question is ill-defined? It is just not possible and thus leaves a sense of dissatisfaction. More important still from the point of view of career development, progress in a career is, perhaps, more than any other single factor, dependent on performance, and other people need a clear view of what this is in your case. As the old maxim has it, 'You must never confuse activity with achievement.' Progress is so often dependent on *evidence* of achievement, and that in turn is dependent on knowing what is expected of you. A job description should not be restrictive; indeed it should be dynamic and if it needs changing and updating regularly, so be it. It is, after all, a working document.

So, in any job you do, make sure you have a clear, written, job description. I would go further: you should have one, everyone who reports to you should have one, and whoever you report to should have one. In fact, the whole process works best if all staff can see each other's job description. That way everyone knows not only what everyone else is doing, but how the various responsibilities inter-relate.

In some organizations this is a difficult area to raise (if, for example, it is seen as unnecessary bureaucracy), but it is worth doing. A job description is of ongoing use as a tool for successful career development.

Obtain the right rewards

Job satisfaction is desirable, important and makes the less attractive parts of any job worthwhile; but it will not pay the rent. Whatever you do, you no doubt expect a fair reward for it. Fair, in this context, normally means a comparison with your peers in the same organization and with those in comparable organizations such as your direct competitors in the commercial world.

A moment's thought shows that money is important in a number of different ways. It is a means of purchasing basic needs (and less basic needs too for that matter!), it is a symbol of the worth the organization places on someone, it is a means of comparison, as stated above, and a reward in itself. But it is not the only reward. Most executive jobs involve increasingly complicated remuneration packages which need consideration before taking a job and during your tenure in it. In addition to your salary, you may receive:

- Company car.
- Pension.
- Incentive or bonus payments.
- Share options.
- Special-terms loans.
- Expenses (that do more than cover the costs incurred in conducting business on behalf of your employer).
- Discounts on company products or services (which will be more valuable in, say, an airline than in a firm manufacturing sewage treatment equipment or some such).
- Health and other insurance.
- Group incentives (e.g. attending an overseas conference).

Some of these may well be linked to performance, and there may be more which you can think of that are favoured in your field of work. Fashions vary with regard to such benefits, and current practice tends to vary in different countries and change over time (as with company cars, much favoured in the UK but nowadays being made much less valuable because of the way they are treated for tax – if you have a company car and have not checked this lately, you would be well advised to do so). Some benefits may have negative sides to them. For example, taking up a special rate loan of some sort may be restrictive – putting you in a position where it is difficult to move without becoming worse off.

Two further points need to be made here. First, do consider other rewards which should perhaps be weighed in the balance. For example, one job may pay less in the long term and yet offer unique training advantages that make it the best choice for the short term, and provide the best chance of moving on in the way you want.

Second, do not be afraid to negotiate these kinds of benefit. Certainly once you reach a certain level, most organizations expect the package to have some element of tailoring. If you do not raise certain issues they may not get an airing at all. Similarly you may want to expand the agenda and include things the company has never even thought about previously. One example of this, which rather appealed to me, concerned an acquaintance of mine seconded to Singapore from London for three years. He was offered a car, but in such a small place where taxis are cheap and plentiful, felt no need for one. Rather, to keep himself independently mobile when necessary, he negotiated a company motorbike! The difference in cost he took as money, an arrangement which suited him well. This might not suit everyone, but it is a good example of someone being kept happy by a policy which accommodates the individual.

A final warning point: negotiation is fine, but you may come to a point where it is better, and more valuable to your future career, not to push further but maintain good relations with those with whom you are negotiating. Principles do not pay the rent, and in some economies it is a real risk to push things so far that your job becomes in doubt. (As negotiation might be regarded as a career development skill, I have written more about the techniques involved in *Conducting Successful Negotiations* [a 'How to Books' paperback].)

Take a chance

Another overall element of your approach to career development involves risk, or the avoidance of it. Here, I am not advocating an approach that throws caution to the wind, and you must consider your temperament and instinctive approach to risk, but chances do sometimes have to be taken. There is an old saying that runs: 'Don't be afraid to go out on a limb if that is where the fruit is.' Trees are high, and climbing may be dangerous, but it makes a fair point. You need to consider this in several ways.

Perception

Your attitude to risk within your job will show, and this, in turn, may influence how you are seen by others in terms of your advancement. How do you want to be seen within your organization? At one end of the scale, there is out and out recklessness which may be linked in others' minds with such characteristics as action being unthinking or ill-considered. Such an image may be wrong for you. So too may be that of a staid, predictable and perhaps, as a result, less innovative person. You must consider where on the scale you should be, and when to make the occasional exception.

Job skills

The degree of risk-taking is something that you have to think about in terms of your job and the action and decisions it demands you take. Some decisions are a risk, and not everything goes right for companies and the people who work in them. Research, consideration and careful decision-making must usually precede any significant action but there is still a place for a chance to be taken. A reputation for a reliable business instinct is good for anyone's image, but when there it is usually balanced by sound homework.

Career decision

We all probably know of people who have taken awful career decisions and gone through a bad patch as a result, and a few who have become stuck in something which they dislike or at least to which they are indifferent. You may be put off a course of action because of the risk, or what you see as a step into unknown territory, and the fear of that clouds the argument in favour of staying put. In my own case, setting up my own business was the best thing I ever did in my career (my mistake, before anyone thinks I am claiming perfection, was not doing it earlier) – but it was also certainly the riskiest.

So you must balance security and good sense, care and consideration in decision-making with those other occasions when you have finally, as it were, to close your eyes and step out into the unknown. To open your eyes and find you are where you want to be is very satisfying. Though it will not always be the right thing to do, or work out if you do it, taking a chance is likely to be something you have to do on occasion. Taking the right ones will surely advance your career.

Get it in writing

Most employers can be trusted; but, realistically, some are not trustworthy (and more may move into circumstances where promises cannot be kept). This may be a small number and it may be for reasons of error or ineptness rather than vindictiveness, but it is worth taking note of. Indeed, the road to the law courts is populated by people who have not done so. Circumstances change: a simple agreement made with the managing director and owner may be worth little five years later when the company has been sold to a multinational conglomerate without a single scruple in any of its many parts.

The moral is that you should have written (and contractual) agreement to your appointment and the terms and conditions that accompany it. Assured by the publishers that this book will be on sale throughout the civilized world, I do not propose to go into detail about employment legislation, which varies a good deal in different locations. However, you should check what makes sense in the environment in which you work (checking twice as carefully if you plan to work in a foreign country), and insist on something appropriate in writing.

The following items may contribute to the contract:

- The details in a letter of appointment.
- A statement of terms and conditions.
- Contents of collective agreements, rules, etc. (in some cases agreed with a trade union or employee body of some sort).
- The custom and practice of the organization.
- Statutory protections (those applying locally).

In Figure 1.1, I have shown a typical list of topics for agreement and written confirmation.

The main statement of terms and conditions should state the following minimum requirements:

1. Who the parties to the contract are (name of the company and the employee).
2. The date when employment began and the date when the employee's period of continuous employment began, taking into account any employment with a previous employer which counts.
3. The scale and method of remuneration, and the intervals at which it will be paid.
4. Hours of work (including any terms and conditions relating to normal working hours).
5. Any entitlement to holidays, including public holidays, and holiday pay.
6. Terms relating to sickness, notification of sickness and pay for sickness.
7. Pension arrangements.
8. The length of notice which an employee is entitled to receive and the amount that must be given if he or she wishes to terminate employment.
9. The title of the job the person is employed to do.
10. Disciplinary rules, or an indication of where the person can go to find out about the rules.
11. The name of the person to whom a grievance should be taken, and the steps or stages of the appeals procedure.

Figure 1.1: Contracts of Employment

This can only be an example and I again urge that you check what is appropriate for you and allow for any special situations. For example, if you are, or become, a director you may wish to have a written list of your legal and financial obligations. You may also feel more comfortable to have a note of any standing instructions relating to a range of items, from business expenses and what may be charged to them, to how a company car may be used. Be sure also that you check the detail; there is a host of factors – periods of notice, maternity arrangements, discipline codes and procedures, insistence on regular medical examinations etc. – which you might want to double-check. Some of these may be important at specific stages of your career. For example, notice-periods if you know you will want to move on before too long, or the effect of a health problem on how you will be treated should it affect your work.

Most of the time such documents are not operationally necessary; if problems or disagreements crop up however, they can be invaluable. Remember also that employment legislation covers many of these areas. There may be a legal requirement bearing on either you or an employer and you may consider it wise to discuss a new contract with a solicitor or specialist in the legal side of personnel before signing.

This is something to get right initially in a job, and to check regularly to ensure everything is up-to-date and appropriate to current circumstances.

Seek sound financial advice

Whatever other reasons there are for working, from satisfaction to philanthropy, clearly for most people money comes high on the list. Now you may not want to maximize earnings in isolation from other benefits. Some jobs offer high rewards but unacceptable terms, conditions or risk, so what you opt to do is often a compromise in this respect. But you are likely not only to want to see a fair return for what you do but make the most of what return you do receive. Thus, unless you are so qualified yourself, you may need a financial adviser.

Now I hope it is not too much of an insult to say that financial advisers are a mixed bunch; some are close relatives of sharks, others are an invaluable asset to any career. They are principally useful in terms of:

- *Tax.* Most tax systems mean that even small complications in your life need careful sorting and, often in such circumstances, if the sorting is not done, you end up paying more tax than is necessary. There is plenty of likelihood of chance affecting arrangements here (from divorce to starting to work partly from home), so it is an area to consider regularly.
- *Investment.* If you do so well in your career that you begin to save significant amounts, then advice as to where you can lodge such money for the best return, and the level of safety that your life demands, may well be useful.

  A crucial area here for most of us is *pensions*. I will resist the temptation to preach the need for an early start (though it is vital), but a reminder of the complications in this area, the changes that can occur during a career to the schemes used, and the way it all works, is worthwhile. For example, people tend to retire (or sometimes have to retire) earlier than in the past.

Others move from full-time employment in one job to self-employment or a portfolio career. Any such development will link to the pension arrangements in place, thus pensions need a greater flexibility than in the past. This is very much an area to know you have buttoned down tight.
- *Complexities.* There is a range of other things that may occur – you could be involved in a profit-sharing scheme, a management buyout or a share option scheme. Again, if you are like me, and not an expert at such things, you may value some advice.

Having said that, you must decide what kind of adviser suits you and then choose carefully. You may consider value in continuity, with one person acting in this role over some years, or want to ring the changes or use several people for different areas of advice. For some, an accountant serves all these roles. My own association with one has proved very useful, sometimes in ways that were difficult to anticipate until they occurred.

Do not be led by events

One of those (American inspired?) business terms that now pervades the English language is the word 'proactive'; everything seems to need a proactive approach or a proactive process. Whatever happened to active? Perhaps the emphasis here should be on the reverse – do not become unthinkingly responsive.

Consider: you have set clear objectives, you have a plan and have thought it all through, then something happens. It may be anything – someone leaves the organization unexpectedly, there is a merger or takeover, a new development, overseas expansion or even a death. It is certainly something you could either not have allowed for in your planning, or something which would have been very difficult to predict in terms of when it might occur. This kind of thing will often need to prompt rapid thinking, but may less often necessitate rapid action.

Of course, there may be times when, unless an opportunity is grasped, it will be gone. In this case, there still needs to be some thinking. You do need to consider all the odds or you may find yourself repenting at leisure. The first task is perhaps to consider whether the urgency is real or apparent.

We all have 20/20 hindsight. It is always easy to look back and judge if something was right or wrong. However, it may be rather more difficult at the time when facts may be limited and the outcome much less clear. I am not sure I can offer a definitive route through this kind of circumstance, except to say most decisions are better and more sure if given a little real thought, and that the temptation to grab, to take a risk in case an opportunity is missed for ever, is great. Perhaps doing your homework – the analysis and planning I have advocated – makes it more likely that you will be able to make good decisions rapidly when the need arises, in which case it is another reason why such planning is worthwhile. Otherwise what seems like a good idea at the time can lead you badly off track and away from your plan and intentions; and that may work out or it may not. An active approach that includes real planning is more likely to cope with the real world, and allow you to deal promptly with any random factors in a way that is most certain to further your career aims.

Be optimistic

I have a theory (entirely unbacked by any statistics!) that optimists tend to do better than pessimists or those who inherently worry about everything. Thinking of this reminds me of a tale from medieval times which makes a valuable point: a servant in the royal household is condemned to life imprisonment for a small misdemeanour. Languishing in his cell, a thought struck him and he sent a message to the king promising that, if he was released, he would work day and night and, within a year, he would teach the king's favourite horse to talk.

This amused the king, and he ordered the courtier to be released and sent to work in the royal stables. The courtier's friends were pleased to see him released, but frightened for him too; after all, horses do not talk, however much training they get. 'What will you do?' they asked. 'So much can happen in a year', he replied; 'I may die, the king may die; or, who knows – the horse may talk!' Who knows indeed. It is a nice story, and I for one hope that by the time the year was up he had thought of some other ruse.

It seems to me that this tale describes the level of optimism to have. Of course, you must never rely on just waiting for something to turn up, and you may be suspicious of the magic formula style of positive mental attitude beloved of many (predominantly American gurus); though you certainly need a high level of self-belief. But if you plan your life and career practically, taking the kinds of views, approaches and actions advocated in this book *and* do so in an optimistic way, that is not only better – you are also likely to be more comfortable with it.

Dealing with success

Having talked about optimism in the last few paragraphs, I think it is right to touch on success early on in the book. The point I want to make is a simple one: do not broadcast your success in an arrogant or unpleasant way. However much you may admire successful people (and want to emulate them), those who crow too stridently about their success are almost universally resented. Modesty is a virtue, as Oliver Hereford said: 'Modesty: the gentle art of enhancing your charm by pretending not to be aware of it'; and there is sense in this, for understatement can be more powerful, especially when an overpowering approach can have the reverse effect to what is intended.

This is true of major factors, like significant promotion, and of smaller successes; no one likes someone who is always crowing just to score points. This leads us to another related point: promotion can mean you are working with people as your subordinates with whom you used to work as colleagues. This can be awkward for both parties, or at least it can feel awkward, and you have to work out a way of dealing with this situation. The right balance is important. You probably can no longer be 'one of the gang' in quite the same way as in the past. But you may find it useful to remain sufficiently close to them to take advantage of the best of the old relationships (importantly without playing favourites) while creating a new basis for the majority of your dealings with the people concerned. If your success is significant, people will know without your overdoing the hype. Some self-publicity is helpful to a career, but it must never be such that it is perceived as arrogant, and by implication, putting others down, or it can easily dilute what should be a positive move.

Everything that has been mentioned so far has a role that can be important individually, but it also sets the scene in terms of giving a feeling about the overall approach and attitude you must adopt to create a continuous focus on career development. In many ways success comes from the details, with many things – as we will continue to see in subsequent pages – contributing to a cumulatively achieved success.

Everything, however, as has already been indicated, contributes more if it stems from and reflects some sound analysis and planning; and it is to this we turn in the next chapter.

2 / Self-analysis

'Success is not the result of spontaneous combustion.
You must first set yourself on fire.'

Fred Shera

THE EARLIEST CAREER PLAN I can remember having in mind for myself was when I was still at school, and that was a desire to be an astronomer. This was born of a passionate interest in the subject rather than any link with my actual or likely abilities. This occurred in an era when the careers master at my school only seemed really well informed when discussing Latin verbs. Once I began to check out what might be necessary, realism soon set in and, though my interest continues, my career took other paths.

Career planning, perhaps sadly, does not mean conjuring up plans that are no more than pie in the sky, but proceeding on a clear, accurate and honest assessment of what might be possible. This means looking inwards. And in this chapter we consider the various forms of self-analysis that can provide a view that acts as a basis for your career development. The link to your aims that this allows will give direction to all your efforts.

Know yourself

Though we all like to think we know ourselves, this may not be entirely true. It is easy to make assumptions, to leave key elements out of the picture. As a result, it is easy to misjudge how your current profile lends itself to career progress, and just what sort of progress may be possible. Assumptions can link to past experience (good and bad), fears, or a host of things. An example of just how much we may misjudge ourselves perhaps makes the point.

As a trainer, one of the things I do regularly is conduct courses designed to improve people's ability to make formal presentations. One category of person who attends (usually told to attend by their employer) has never done this, or has done very little of it. They hate the thought of it because they think they cannot do it well, and would much prefer to avoid the whole subject and the task. Yet these same people, or certainly many of them, prove to be quick and effective at learning how to do a good job on a presentation. They find there is a difference between not knowing how to go about something and inherently not being able to do it. With the knowledge of how to tackle it, and with practice, something like this, initially daunting, can be successfully added to their list of skills. Yet previously they may have been avoiding tasks, jobs, even promotion, that were likely to put them in a position where they would have to do this seemingly worrying task. Sometimes you may note things as negative – 'I can't do that' – when they should be noted as 'could do', even if time and effort of some sort is necessary to make it possible.

There may well be aspects of your nature and ability you think about in this way, so the first step to deciding a route forward is to look at where you are at the moment. This should be done systematically and honestly, and you may find it useful to keep some notes of what the thinking produces. The next sections lead you through a suitable progression of self-analysis.

Assess your skills

Leaving aside what you cannot do, you might be surprised at how many skills you already have. Remember that it is quite possible that things you do and take for granted, you can only in fact do because of considerable, and perhaps unusual, experience. So all the things for which you have aptitude you should list. Some general headings under which to group your abilities might include:

- *Communicating*: everything from writing a report to issuing instructions.
- *Influencing:* that includes persuading, negotiating and promoting ideas.
- *Managing:* everything to do with managing other people.
- *Problem-solving:* analysing and drawing conclusions and coming up with solutions.
- *Creativity:* generating ideas, seeing things in the round, having an open mind.
- *Social skills:* not just relating to people but having insight, helping others, facilitating.
- *Numerical:* figures, statistics, accounts and, these days, computers.

- *Administration:* everything from running a tight ship and attention to detail, to thorough project management.
- *Special skills:* here such skills as speaking a foreign language, computer literacy, unusual technical skills, etc. should be mentioned.

At any stage of your career, you should have this full picture in mind and therefore documented. The form in Figure 2.1 shows how you might make some notes about yourself.

Communicating

Influencing

Managing

Problem-solving

Creativity

Social skills

Numerical skills

Administrative skills

Special skills

Figure 2.1: Assess your skills

It would be an interesting exercise to compile such a list now, and again later when you have read the whole book. Some of the topics listed above will recur as headings in their own right, and you may view things differently after a review of how important some of the skill areas are from a career point of view.

Assess your work values

It is not enough to know what skills you have. These must be viewed in the light of your work values. Do you, for instance, have:

- A strong need to achieve?
- A need for a high salary?
- High work interest requirements?
- A liking for doing something worthwhile?
- A desire to do something creative?
- Specific requirements (such as to travel, to be independent, innovative or part of a team)?

A wide range of permutations may be involved here and they may change over time. For example, travel may be attractive if you are young and single, but become less so if or when you have young children, and then may become more attractive again in future when a family is older.

Figure 2.2 opposite shows how you can document this area; you can usefully mark the centre column, say out of ten.

Assess your personal characteristics

Though acquiring new skills can affect things, most people do not radically change their habits and ways, at least not dramatically and certainly not without effort, once they are old enough to be into a career. You need to assess yourself in this respect and do so honestly. Are you innovative, positive, optimistic, hard working, prepared to take risks? What sort of a person, in fact, are you? There may be a clash here. In thinking through your work values, you may feel that you are suited to, and want to be involved in, something with considerable cut and thrust, innovating, creative and generally working at the leading edge. But an honest assessment of yourself may show that, whatever the superficial or status attraction of this option, it is just not really you. Risk-taking is not your

Work value	How important is this?	Remarks

Figure 2.2: Assess your work values

thing and a different, perhaps more supportive role is where you are most likely to excel.

Again you should list what you feel is relevant about yourself here; see Figure 2.3 overleaf.

Assess your non-work characteristics

One way or another, work and social life have to coexist alongside each other. They may do so peaceably, or there may be conflicts between them (and stress because of this clash is a current issue in business life). It is not automatically necessary to career success to be a workaholic, though a strictly 9-to-5 attitude to the job is perhaps

Personal characteristic	Relevance to job

Figure 2.3: Assess your personal characteristics

not recommended either. And on the positive side, work and interests or hobbies may overlap constructively, the one teaching you something about the other.

There are questions to be asked here too:

- What are your family circumstances?
- Where do you need/want to live?
- How much time can you spend away from home?
- What are your other responsibilities and interests?

Family

If you have a partner, wife or husband then priorities may need to be set, because the career-building priorities of one can clash with the other or with the family as a whole. It is, sadly, perfectly possible to arrive successfully at the top of the heap – a success in business, but with home, family and happiness in ruins. This may sound dramatic, but the issues here are worth some serious thought. Not least, there are times when career decisions must be made fast or opportunities will be lost. If the relationship between home, family and work has never been discussed, then the man who comes home from the office to tell his wife: 'I have this great new opportunity with the company, but it means living in Hong Kong for two years', is in for some heated debate. And these days, with both partners so often working and women increasingly having their own careers, such debate may be started by the wife saying something similar. If either has promised to go back to the office the next day with a decision, the complications are likely to escalate.

Interests

Interests are an important issue. All work and no play is, for most people, a bad thing. You need to look at your interests and hobbies alongside your job and your future career intentions. Such may involve a wide range of activities or intentions, from a passion for sailing to a desire to stand for the local council. Can job and interests move forward together? How much time do you want to put in to both hobbies and work? These are not easy questions and must be worked out over a period of time. Even so there may come times when there are clashes. If you have thought it all through and discussed it with other family members as appropriate, then transient problems are more likely to be just that – transient.

There are no right or wrong answers here and I would not presume to give advice – only you can decide the relationship and the balance that is right for you. The amount of time and energy a job needs to take up and what must be left for other things varies between individuals and rightly so; it would be a dull old world if we were all the same.

The smooth planning of these issues certainly helps you make career decisions more easily and more promptly than would otherwise be the case. And for most, success in life means career and private life working reasonably compatibly together, whatever the

Non-work characteristic	Compatibility with job

Figure 2.4: Assess your non-work characteristics

demands of the job at any particular moment. Figure 2.4 suggests how you can document this area.

Have the ideal job in mind

All the thinking about your skills, circumstances and interests should enable you to produce a picture of the ideal job – that is *your* ideal job. While you should recognize that the ideal may realistically never be achieved, this is no reason not to aim for something as close as possible to whatever your ideal may be.

Consider particularly:

• The area of work you want to be in – the tasks, responsibilities etc.
• The kind of people situation you want to be in – many/few, managing others or not, in a team etc.

- The kind of working environment you want – a large organization, a big city, many facilities etc.
- Where and how you want to live – location, travel etc.
- The rewards you want – salary and other benefits.

As with the areas previously reviewed, here again you should make some notes of the thinking you go through and the conclusions you draw. See Figure 2.5.

'Ideal' area of work

'Ideal' people situation

'Ideal' work environment

'Ideal' rewards

Figure 2.5: Your 'ideal' job

All the information assembled to date forms the basis for much of the subsequent thinking that is necessary as you consider how you may take action through the way you work, and what you think and do so as to build your career successfully. Opportunities and your real circumstances constantly have to be compared. Some career paths will play to your strengths, others will not, and some will cause a clash of objectives that will be problematical. Others will simply not be open to you because of your mix of talents and abilities (though this latter is something you can work at correcting).

The picture you build up here is solely for your own benefit. Some of the facts and information may also be useful at appraisals and in the documentation and discussion that may be necessary if you wish to change employer. These are issues dealt with later in the book.

In addition to this self-analysis, you may, on occasion, find it useful to add an additional dimension to the process.

Professional career guidance

Sometimes, the problem arises that as you try to analyse both yourself and the path you want to take, you can come to no real conclusion as to what will suit you best in the future. In this case, it may be worth seeking assistance. Talking it through with a friend, perhaps a more experienced one, may be all that is necessary. Two heads are sometimes better than one. On other occasions professional assistance may be called for. An example of such a circumstance may make the point clearer.

I came from a background that had no links with the commercial or business world. My father was in the medical profession and once he had got over the shock of my wanting to go into 'industry', insisted that I should first go to an organization (in London) called the Vocational Guidance Association. This body uses psychometric tests to measure the aptitudes of a person and matches them to the type of job and career that seems most suited to the individual concerned. As my father was paying, I agreed to go, and found myself subjected to a battery of tests that lasted, as I recall, most of the day. I returned home and a report cataloguing what little ability I had at that stage arrived a few days later.

To cut a long story short, I did go into industry (publishing) and cannot now remember what difference, if any, the report made. What I do remember is finding it many years later when I moved house. It described the nature of the job they had felt I would most enjoy, and I found it matched exactly those things which I was involved in at that time. I have always had a greater respect for such services since. An objective view is sometimes useful, and while there is no test that will magically put you into a career where success will follow inevitably because the match between you and what you are doing is so good that there is no other possible result, the prompt to your thinking such analysis can provide may be very useful.

Such services are available in most large cities and they are by no means only designed for those moving from education to a first job (the time I did my tests), but can be useful at any stage of a career where you wish to check how your plan is progressing and whether you are going in a direction that is likely to produce job satisfaction – or indeed whether you should change direction. Choose a good adviser (by no means everyone who offers career advice and testing is good) and this may be for some a useful check at a particular stage of their career.

You may also meet such tests as part of some potential future employer's interview-and-selection procedure. Tried and tested measures may be useful and might be regarded as a sign of care being taken over selection; though watch out for pseudo tests that may only indicate that the selector is clutching at straws in an ill-judged attempt to make a good choice. If you want to understand more about how such tests work, and how in an interview situation you might survive them or impress with them, *How to Succeed in Psychometric Tests* by David Cohen is a good reference.

The next step is to link the findings of whatever analysis you undertake to the way in which you will develop your career, and do so in a way that is of practical help to the process.

Match your analysis of yourself with market demands

Whatever picture your various self-analysis exercises build up, it must be matched realistically with the demands made by employers in the marketplace. Let me put that more specifically: it must match up with the demands made by employers in the section of industry or other organization in which you intend to excel. So, whilst there are perhaps generally desirable characteristics that we might list: being adaptable to change (or able to prompt it), flexible, thorough or productive and so on, there will be more specific characteristics in terms of abilities and nature which will be demanded in a particular field.

Indeed, a certain characteristic may be an asset in one area and frowned on in another, as something like creativity might be differently regarded in an advertising agency and a more traditional business. Similarly, what for some is drive and initiative, others will regard as aggressive and self-seeking.

Two points arise from this. First, having analysed yourself and your intended field (even if you are already in it), you must aim to cultivate the kind of profile likely to contribute to success in that field. Or, for some, react to analysis which shows that all the signs

are that you are *not* well suited in a way that enhances the possibility of success in a particular area. The better the match, the better the
chances that your profile will allow you to do well, and progress
along your chosen path.

But a good match is not, of itself, sufficient; there is a second
point here which an anecdote will perhaps serve to illustrate. A good
friend has a son who has just left acting college and is intent on carv-
ing out a career on the stage. I went to see a play he was in at a small
London fringe theatre: a production in which the cast were all
young people starting out on their careers. His performance seemed
to me excellent, and I said as much to my friend later. 'What else did
you notice?' he asked and, when I could not think what he meant,
he commented, 'The whole of the cast was excellent.' His point was
that talent was not going to be the only factor in any success his son
might achieve. He would have to get ahead of a strong field to rise to
the rank of star. So it is in many fields; and certainly this applies
equally to industry. Just having the right qualifications and aptitudes is rarely sufficient – others have them too – you have to have
them in the right amount and at the right level; and they must show.
Then, with some luck and if you work at it, you may carve out success for yourself. But never make the mistake of thinking this
happens in a vacuum – it happens with others around you trying to
do similar things. Knowing how well you match up is, nevertheless,
a good starting point – one worth some thought.

Sum up your analysis in clear objectives

Every management guru has their own version of the premise that
every business must have a plan or, as it is sometimes put, 'If you do
not know where you are going, any road will do.' It is true, it does
make a difference; as with any business, so with any career. This really is common sense, and yet conversely it is so very easy to wake up
one day and discover that what we have been wont to regard as planning is in fact no more than bowing to the inevitable and, if it looks
good, taking the credit for it.

Having said that objectives are important, another point should
be made: they must be flexible. Life in all its aspects, certainly in
business, is dynamic. Objectives cannot be allowed to act as a strait-
jacket, yet we need their guidance. Having them and being sure they
are clear adds direction to even the best plan.

In business, people talk of 'rolling' plans. This means a plan that is reasonably clear and comprehensive for the shorter term, then sets out broad guidelines beyond that and, further ahead, has only main elements clearly stated. As time goes by, the plan can be updated and advanced into the future. What was year three, say, becomes year two and the detail that can be laid against it fills out. With your own career in mind, you will find a similar approach works well. In the short term, when you can anticipate more clearly what may happen, the detail of how you intend to proceed is clearer; further ahead you have notes on the outline strategy and key issues.

Remembering to say 'My objective is to become a marketing director' is not much help without some clear actions and steps along the way. Objectives should be SMART. This well-known mnemonic, much quoted in the training world, stands for Specific, Measurable, Achievable, Realistic and Timed, thus:

- *Specific* – expressed clearly and precisely.
- *Measurable* – it must be possible to tell if you have achieved it (the difference between saying you want to be 'very successful' or 'marketing director').
- *Achievable* – it must not be so difficult as to be pie in the sky, otherwise the plan that goes with it similarly becomes invalid and of no practical help in taking things forward.
- *Realistic* – it must fit with your self-analysis and be what you want; it might be a valid objective to aim for something possible but not ideal (promotion might be possible within a department, but your real intention is to get out beyond that) but this will not be helpful. Action is needed with more ambitious objectives in mind.
- *Timed* – this is important; objectives are not to be achieved 'eventually', but by a particular moment: when do you aim to be marketing director – this year, next year or when?

To sum up: there is no need for elaborate documentation here. Any objectives and any plans are purely for your own guidance, but a few notes on paper are likely to be useful – as we have seen there is just too much here to consider (and update) for it to be kept safely in your head. In addition, there are times (such as appraisal or when training is contemplated) when it may be useful to think of current events alongside the notes you have made. If you not only know which road you should be on, but have taken steps to make sure you go purposively along it, that is a good start to the overall process of career development. Indeed, most of what we will touch on during the remaining text can usefully be considered with your own view of yourself clearly in mind.

Never cut off your options

I think this is one of the most sensible and useful pieces of advice I have ever been given in this area. Realistically the options you have, indeed the options you build into your career plan, are more like a river constantly branching into tributaries than one straight road. There is rarely advantage in rejecting privately or taking action that rules out any particular path. Unless you are genuinely clairvoyant (in which case what are you doing reading this: you *know* what level of success you will achieve!) you never know in advance which will be the best route; or afterwards for that matter. Circumstances change. What seemed like a long shot suddenly becomes a real possibility, or what seems secondary becomes your best option; provided you have not ruled it out. So keep all your options open and only do away with one for a good reason (it is possible sacrificing one will open up another, and perhaps a better one, but this should be a conscious decision).

Career planning has a good deal in common with strategy (to be absolutely clear remember that objectives are 'desired results', and strategy is the 'course of action adopted to achieve that result'). You need to take a strategic view, and the rule discussed here is in fact just one aspect of this process. At the risk of introducing yet another topic you need to know about, you could do worse than to read a little about strategy and, if you want to give business books a rest for a moment, read James Clavell's adventure story about Japan, the novel *Shogun*. It has more in it about strategy than most titles with the word 'strategy' in the title (and it is an enthralling read).

3 / People Power

'To escape criticism – do nothing, say nothing, be nothing.'
Elbert Hubbard

TAKE THE PEOPLE out of business and there is little left. People issues show themselves in many ways and there is an overlap here between this and communication and management, both dealt with later. Career development is an interactive process, it is not something you can do in isolation. So, here we review a number of people factors that, whether simple or more complex, must not be forgotten and which can all potentially assist practically with making your career development activity successful.

Keep a people file

Problems, opportunities and people go together. So often when something crops up and you need information, assistance or advice, the first thought that comes to mind is related to a person: 'They'll know', you say to yourself, and then you think again. You can see them in your mind's eye. You know you met them at that conference you attended in Cambridge, or was it Oxford? You had a meal together, you . . . but what was their name? What company did they work for? Where is their business card? You cannot find the name, and something that might have been sorted in two minutes on the telephone ends up taking an hour.

We all do it.

In some ways, no great harm is done. After all, you cannot keep in touch with everyone and it is difficult to know who will be useful to remember or know in five years' time (remember career development is a long-term process). But it is probably better to note too many names than to miss good ones. They may prove useful (or just pleasant) to know in all sorts of ways; not least with an eye on career development.

Therefore, you need a people file.

This is a little more than an address book or a file for business cards (or, these days, it may be computerized or in a personal electronic organizer). It needs to record some information about each person, enough so that you can call something to mind about them. For instance, record:

- The date you met.
- Where you met.
- The circumstances of meeting (did you sit next to them on a flight or meet them at a conference?).
- Whether you were introduced by a third party (and if so, who that person was).
- Keep their name, position, company, address, etc. and also maybe something about them ('Knows all about regression analysis', 'Is well connected with large financial services firms' or even 'Can recommend a good restaurant in New York').

There can be no half measures here. It must be done systematically, it must be done regularly (it is amazing how quickly some of the detail about someone is forgotten) and it must include everyone that may be useful in the future. You can always prune it a little over the months and years so that it remains manageable. There is an old saying 'It is not *what* you know, but *who* you know' that matters in life. If there is any truth in this (and there must be) you have to know who you know. Such a system is not an option in career development, it is a prerequisite.

Use networking

Before we networked, we kept in touch. It is no good having a good network of contacts, safely noted (as above) and then not keeping them 'live'. You have to keep in touch. It matters less how this is done than that it should happen. The frequency will vary among your list of contacts: some only need a card once a year, at Christmas or New Year perhaps, others need to be called a couple of times every month. And some will contribute to the frequency of contact by contacting you; networking is a two-way street.

Sometimes the contact is social, sometimes it is based on a specific request for help and information, sometimes it is unashamed brain-picking. Before he retired, I used to see an American consultant regularly. He would phone up and say he was in town and suggest a lunch or, more often, breakfast. He was a nice guy and it was always good to see him. It was also enormously stimulating. He could pack more ideas, more creative thinking and more examples to back up points made into what was essentially a social contact than anyone I have ever met. An hour and a half with him was like a mini-seminar and it was tiring, you did not realize how much you were thinking and concentrating until you came away from the session. I learnt a great deal from him over the years. But he did too, he was an unashamed brain-picker of the highest order. Good networking is like this. It is interesting, it is fun, and yet we learn from it and thus keeping up with people can be a constructive process.

Internally networking often has little to do with the classic organizational hierarchy. Your network can go up, down and sideways; and you should work at making sure it does exactly that. One contact often leads to another and you may be surprised at the contacts that can be created.

The only down side is that the processes involved are time-consuming, and you have to balance the need to keep your contacts live with the other time pressures in your job and in your life generally. One thing is certain: the old principle of two heads being better than one can work well, so this activity can pay dividends – speaking for myself I have received three unsolicited job offers from such contacts over my career, and I accepted two of them! Think of the range of people who might help your career and the different ways in which this might occur. Some are advice-givers, others know others they can put you in touch with, some – as I have suggested – may link specifically to career enhancement. If they do not offer you a job, they know the best time to approach someone else or they suggest you get to grips with some new skill that proves vital as your career progresses.

Mix in the right circles

So far, comments have been made about people who you know, keeping a note of them and keeping in touch. Now we turn to how you get to know them in the first place, or at least some of them. You need to work at cultivating contacts. Just where and how this is done will depend on the nature of your job and the kind of business you are in, but some general principles apply.

Internally you need to take an interest in the organization at large – who does what, who runs what and who knows what. Most organizations have an informal communications network which is as important as the formal structure (this includes the ubiquitous grapevine which will come up again in Chapter 4 (Communications), and this means that in a large organization there is quite a bit of ground to cover. On the basis that you only get out of something what you put in, it is worth seeking opportunities to contribute in ways that allow you to mix with the right people. What committees, working parties and project teams should you be on? Some will be very useful, putting you in touch with the prime movers and giving you an opportunity to demonstrate your competence. Others are a waste of time. And what is more, if you get a reputation for being perpetually in such groups it will not do your credibility any good at all. Some will be contentious, and you may have to consider the wisdom of being part of the team that moved the office from its prestigious quarters into what many regard as a slum on some distant industrial estate, even if it did save a great deal of money. You can no doubt think of other examples. Such well-chosen activity is sensible and useful.

Externally the same kind of thinking applies. For example, what should you belong to and participate in – the local management institute, trade, professional or technical bodies, or other interest groups, clubs? There may be sense in being involved in some things from all or some of these categories. Again pick carefully, and get involved where this is more useful than simply belonging and turning up at meetings. In doing this, always work out an order of priorities as you are unlikely to be able to do everything; indeed the balance is important and it is not being suggested that such things take over your life or take up a disproportional amount of time – that would be self-defeating. It is, however, an area that stands regular review to check how time is spent and what is most useful in order to change and adapt what you do. Do not, for instance, fall into the trap of letting things that are fun squeeze out things that are useful; though it is, of course, nice if some such are fun.

The moral here is that just sitting in your office, even if you are doing an excellent job, does not give you such a high profile as operating and being seen to operate across a wider canvas. When opportunities come up, perhaps in discussion, among a group of senior managers where you want your credentials to come readily to mind, it helps to be in those minds, preferably filed in a number of different places. The first necessity, before any new opportunity is likely to be aimed your way, is quite simple – for people, the right people to remember you.

Recruit a mentor

One of the motivations for a manager, or at least for some managers, is the satisfaction of helping other people develop and of seeing them do well. I was, looking back, very lucky in that two of the people I worked for very early in my career were like this. I learned a great deal from both and learned it very much quicker than would otherwise have been the case. I am not, on the other hand, at all sure that if I had not this luck I would have had the wits to seek out such assistance, my career planning was too naive in those days.

Organizing assistance from others in furthering your career may involve many people, but some may be especially important. The modern name for such helpers is 'mentor'. The ideal mentor is sufficiently senior to have knowledge, experience and clout. They need the process to appeal to them, and they need to have time to put into the process; this need not be great, the key thing is that they have the willingness to spend some time regularly helping someone else. If your boss and your mentor are one and the same person, that might be ideal, but it is not essential. Usually, if such a relationship lasts, it will start out one-way – they help you – and become more two-way over the years; perhaps the person on the mentor side makes the decision to help rather on the basis of this anticipated possibility.

After the first few years of a career, there is no reason why you cannot have regular contact with a number of people where in each case the relationship is of this nature. This can take various forms. In my own case, for instance, my work in marketing overlaps sometimes with the area of market research. While I know a good deal about aspects of this, certainly in terms of what can be done with it, I have no real strength in certain of the specialist techniques involved (such as questionnaire design). But I have a research mentor – someone who can help and advise me in this particular field. This is very useful and works on the basis of a swap, in other words he helps in that way and I am able (I hope and believe) to advise and assist him in other ways. This is a not uncommon basis, can be very useful and is well worth cultivating.

This kind of thing should be regarded as really very different from, and very much more than, simple networking. The nature and depth of the interaction and the time and regularity of it is much more extensive. This is not primarily a career assistance process in the sense of someone who will give you a leg up the organization through recommendation or lobbying, though this can of course occur. It is more important in helping develop the range and depth of your competences which in turn can act to boost your career.

As a final example, my business partner is someone who makes an art form of this kind of role, for example I know very well I would not do the writing work which is now a regular part of my portfolio (including this book!) if it was not for his regular help and cajoling! It makes a difference, and a very positive one at that.

Let your secretary help

Do you have a secretary? If the answer is no, then the sooner you can organize to have one the better. If you do, or when you get one, make absolutely sure that you get an efficient one; and then work at the relationship, because without any doubt a good secretary is a person who can be a decided and positive career asset. Being a 'good secretary' sounds straightforward enough. However, the ideal characteristics are daunting to say the least. The role demands administrative efficiency, sound writing skills (backed up by good typing, shorthand and computer and/or word processing skills), and the ability to cope with a growing range of office equipment from fax to modem. In addition, she (it is most often, but not always, a she) must be hard working, numerate, tactful, persistent, charming, and committed – that report will not be ready in 24 hours just because she is paid to do it. And it helps if she is clairvoyant, has a memory like a computer, two pairs of hands, the patience of a saint and is fluent in several languages including whichever one is lurking somewhere within her boss's illegible handwriting.

Given support, which includes everything from not blaming things on her – 'My secretary forgot to remind me' – to taking time to communicate and tell her what is going on, why, and how things need to work out and therefore be handled, a good and involved secretary can not only help you do your job better, but be a great career-boosting asset. One point before investigating this further. Secretaries seem to be a widely under-utilized resource. Amongst other topics, I sometimes conduct courses on time management. On these, indeed on any management course, I have yet to meet an executive who says he has sufficient time. Yet on courses I run for groups of secretaries, they will all speak of the many things that their managers do that they could perfectly well cope with if allowed. On management programmes, however, if it is suggested that more is delegated to secretaries there always seem to be reasons why not – 'I am not sure they could really understand . . .'

So make sure that you really use your secretary's talents fully. A good secretary reflects well on the person (or people, because secretaries are sometimes shared) for whom she works, and is able to help create an aura of efficiency about the office, and the activity in the office. Perhaps almost more important, she can be an ambassador for you, particularly in your absence, supporting decisions and policies, helping send out the informal messages that help create an image. And, of course, making sure that work and projects are progressing as you would want (this is one of the reasons communication is so important; if she does not know your aims she cannot help achieve them). I once heard a nice story about a secretary to a senior industrialist who seemed to spend most of his time travelling abroad. During one of his many absences a colleague came into his office to see him and, discovering he was away, asked: 'Who does all his work while he is overseas?' His secretary scarcely hesitated before replying: 'The same person who does it when he is here!' There is much truth in this. A good secretary increases your productivity, efficiency and visibility. Never take her loyalty and assistance for granted, and work at making her and her role a real asset.

A two-way street

There is a danger that some of the suggestions of this section, keeping a people file, networking, and so on, may seem somewhat soulless and one-sided. This need not be so, and what you can achieve in these ways will be minimized if you see it like that. The simplest way of injecting a two-way element into these dealings is to remember to thank those who offer assistance, whether it is advice, or something more tangible. For a start, this is just common courtesy. It is appreciated, and makes it more likely that those others involved will be disposed to help you again. A written note is often more appropriate than simply a word, especially when directed at the older generation.

Secondly, this kind of assistance is itself a two-way street. You will be more able to obtain the further assistance you need if you return any favours; indeed not only is it useful to have the reputation for being a ready source of assistance for others, the whole process actually becomes more interesting and satisfying. In a busy life it is all too easy to lose touch, not get back to people or otherwise put good networking relationships at risk. Sit back and think – who do you owe a 'Thank you' to?

Because any organization is dependent on people, so is the process of thriving in one. Use people to help your career development, select and involve the right people, but be sure to give as much as you receive.

The next chapter focuses on communication, which is again inherently involved with people.

4 Communication and Communicating

'It's what you learn after you know it all that counts.'

John Wooden

MOST OF WHAT GOES ON in business and around organizations is, in fact, communications; and anything that is not communications is probably dependent on something that is to initiate it or keep it going. If you are in business then you are in communications. Your ability to communicate and the way in which you do so is so important to your career that here it is reviewed in its own chapter, though it is certainly one of a number of career and management skills of which more are dealt with elsewhere.

Communication is difficult

The first step to using good communications to further your career is to recognize the difficulties it presents and resolve to work at avoiding them; more than that, you should resolve to excel at communications. Perhaps I may start my comment on this by quoting from the Preface of my earlier book *Agreed!*

As a busy manager you communicate all the time – verbally, in writing, with a variety of people – and do so perfectly well most of the time. Occasionally, however, you will find someone asking, 'What do you mean?' in response to something which you have said. Sometimes you initiate the correction – 'What I meant was . . .', and sometimes people will say to you: 'You want me to do *what*?' As you can see, communication is not always as easy as it seems.

Communication can suffer from being unclear – '. . . you fit the thing onto that sprocket thing and . . .' (just try it). Or imprecise – '. . . then it's about a mile' (three miles later . . .). It can be so full of jargon that we find ourselves referring to a manual excavation device, instead of calling a spade a spade. Or it can be 'gobbledegook': 'Considerable difficulty has been encountered in the selection of optimum materials and experimental methods but this problem is being attacked vigorously and we expect the development phase will proceed at a satisfactory rate.' ('We are looking at the handbook and trying to decide what to do.') So much so that the sense is diluted. There are innumerable barriers to communication, not least the assumptions, prejudices and inattention of those on the receiving end.

All this may simply cause a bit of confusion and take a moment to sort out, or it can cause major problems either immediately or later. Never is there more likely to be problems than when there is an intention to get someone to do something. Not only has the message got to be particularly clear but, because the days of saying 'Do this' to anyone in most organizations have long since gone, often communication needs to be *persuasive*.

If you are going to work with people and you are going to get things done, you need to communicate clearly and, very often, persuasively. What is more, you need to be seen to do so. Your communication breakdowns, if any, can cause problems for others, something that is hardly likely to mark you out as a high flyer. Your communications successes label you as competent, capable and – on occasion – mark out your abilities as excellent. Any such successes are disproportionately important as excellence in communication may well be read by others as indicating a broader competence. And the need to persuade, getting your own way, particularly being able to obtain support for decisions and action that prove successful, is simply vital. Few careers really progress without some strength in this area. So, with this in mind, let us examine the most important aspects of this fact.

Communicate clearly

Crystal clarity should be the aim of all your communication. (It goes without saying, at least in this section, that if you are going to communicate you have to have something worthwhile to say – assuming that, whatever it is must be made clear.) We have already highlighted the inherent difficulty of successful communication. If you want to guarantee to make your communications clear and surmount those difficulties, you need to actively take a considered approach – much communications failure occurs because there is an assumption that there is no need for thought. As luck would have it, prevailing standards are on your side because every office in the world tends to be witness to regular communications breakdown. Habit and prevailing style can compound the problem with office-speak and gobbledegook, bureaucracy, jargon and unnecessary complexity dressed up as substance, all combining to obscure any meaning that may lurk within the confusion.

You can probably think of examples in your own office, at meetings, in memos, or just in conversation over coffee where you come away saying: 'What was all that about?' A classic example is a much-circulated office memo, all too probably based on fact, which purports to mark the progress of some project or other. This was dipped into earlier and is shown in full below.

Standard Progress Report
For Those with No Progress to Report

During the survey period which ends 14 February, considerable progress has been made in the preliminary work directed towards the establishment of the initial activities. [*We are getting ready to start, but we have not done anything yet.*] The background information has been surveyed and the functional structure of the component parts of the cognizant organization has been clarified. [*We looked at the project and decided that George would lead it.*]

Considerable difficulty has been encountered in the selection of optimum approaches and methods but this problem is being attacked vigorously and we expect the development phase will proceed at a satisfactory rate. [*George is looking through the handbook.*] In order to prevent unnecessary duplication of previous efforts in the same field, it was necessary to establish a survey team which has conducted a rather extensive tour through various departments with immediate access to the system. [*George and Harry had a nice time visiting everyone.*]

The Steering Committee held its regular meeting and considered rather important policy matters pertaining to the overall organizational levels of the line and staff responsibilities that devolve on the personnel associated with the specific assignments resulting from the broad functional specifications [*untranslatable – sorry*]. It is believed that the rate of progress will continue to accelerate as necessary personnel are made available for the necessary discussions. [*We will get some work done as soon as we find somebody who knows something.*]

As a result, things are delayed, communication takes up more time than it should and, at worst, mistakes are made and things go wrong. The career-minded can simply not afford to be like this, because the fact is that individuals are inextricably linked to, and characterized by, their communication style. If you are clear, really clear, then you stand out in this sea of confusion, and do so to your advantage.

Think of the impact of clarity: a clear succinct summary in a report or proposal, a complex sequence of events spelt out so that the key elements shine forth, a plan, policy or procedure that all can understand first time – these are all noticeable to their recipients. If people expect something to be complicated, then there can be real surprise and pleasure in finding that it is, in fact, straightforward.

If a message has what psychologists call a high cognitive cost – in other words it gives the impression that it will be difficult – then its likely usefulness is downgraded even before any real attempt is made to take it on board. Think of something like the instructions for a video recorder, for many people just opening it at random lets it shout at you: 'This is going to be difficult.' Anything that stands out because they make understanding easy for those to whom the communication is directed is appreciated. So too with people. If you can communicate clearly and do it consistently in your job, and get a reputation for so doing, it creates a powerful feeling of confidence in your abilities. A poor plan well explained is not as good as a good plan well explained, but both are likely to do better than a poor plan poorly explained. So, if you have to respond to recommendations designed to improve efficiency by rearranging the office layout, do not say: 'Man machine interface requirements in the system environment impose restrictive visual acuity problems on word-processing activity.' Say, 'But it is arranged so that the secretary cannot see the VDU screen.'

The checklist in Figure 4.1 sets out the principles of clear communication; it is a task you must learn to undertake consistently well in whatever form – report, memo, meeting and more.

1. Choose the appropriate medium: verbal, written – report, letter, memo, fax.
2. Be clear in your own mind what the objective of any communication really is.
3. Put your message in a form that suits the intended recipient. Remember misunderstanding is all too easy to create. Therefore aim for simplicity and put things succinctly. Avoid jargon and confusing words.
4. Match what you put over to the level of experience and understanding of the recipient.
5. Aim to create and maintain interest (people will not understand if they do not listen properly).
6. Select the right time, and avoid distractions.
7. Be practical (total lack of realism will be rejected out of hand).
8. Watch for signs of how something is being received (and adjust what you say as necessary).

Figure 4.1: Making a message clear

Listen (really listen)

Communication is a two-way street. The way you put any message over is important, but it is also important how you respond. One key response to other people's communication is to listen. It is always a compliment to be described as a 'good listener'.

Listening, and being prepared to listen, makes an impression. And, of course, the immediate feedback that it provides will help you to gain accurate understanding and manage any conversation better. But there is listening, and there is listening. The trouble is that the mind can listen faster than people can speak – yes, literally. This means that the mind has time to wander off as you listen (often preparing what you are going to say next, especially if it is contra-dictory) and it tends to do just that; so listening becomes inefficient. The result? The all too frequent: 'Sorry, what did you say?' which can signal not simply inattention, but lack of interest, and this alone is sufficient to begin to get two people at cross-purposes.

So, listening is vital. You must resolve to be a good listener – an *active* listener.

The checklist (Figure 4.2) suggests some ways to approach this.

1. *Want to listen*. This is easy once you realize how useful it is to the communication process.
2. *Look like a good listener*. If people can see they have your attention, feedback will be more forthcoming.
3. *Understand*. It is not just the words but what lies behind them that you must note.
4. *React*. Let people see that you have heard, understood and are interested. Nods, small comments etc. will encourage.
5. *Stop talking*. Other than small acknowledgements, you cannot talk and listen at the same time. Do not interrupt.
6. *Use empathy*. Put yourself in the other person's shoes and make sure you really appreciate their point of view.
7. *Check*. If necessary, ask questions to clarify matters as the conversation proceeds. An understanding based even partly on guesses is dangerous. But ask questions diplomatically, do not say 'You didn't explain that properly'.
8. *Remain unemotional*. Too much thinking ahead ('However can I overcome that objection?') can distract you.
9. *Concentrate*. Allow nothing to distract you.
10. *Look at the speaker*. Nothing is read more rapidly as disinterest than an inadequate focus of attention.
11. *Note particularly key points*. Edit what you need to retain key points manageably.
12. *Avoid personalities*. Do not let your view of an individual distract you from the message.
13. *Do not lose yourself in subsequent argument*. Some thinking ahead may be useful; too much and you suddenly may find you have missed something.
14. *Avoid negatives*. To begin with at least, signs of disagreement (even a look) can make the other person clam up.
15. *Make notes*. Do not trust your memory, and if it is polite to do so, ask permission.

Figure 4.2: Active listening checklist

The result is worth striving for, as really listening gives you the edge in conversation and labels you as a sensitive communicator. And, as has been said, everything that builds your ability to be, and to be seen to be a good communicator, is valuable in career terms. It not only means you are likely to be able to do your job better, it means you are more likely to be consulted, approached, involved, networking is easier and your profile moves up a notch.

Seek and watch for feedback

Listening, referred to above, is only one, albeit major, form of feedback in communication. You will only be a good communicator if you resolve to note and use all the signs given by others and work at doing so. This implies a number of things. You should:

- watch for visible signs (gestures, expressions, etc.);
- listen for non-verbal signs (things not said but sounded, such as a grunt of disapproval or a tut of impatience);
- ask questions (itself a skill worth cultivating);
- read between the lines – in speech as well as in writing – to see what may be really meant. As I am sure you have noticed, people do not always say what they mean; thus a sentence that begins, 'With the greatest respect . . .' is usually followed by an argument that respects the other party very little if at all.

All this and more will put you in a better position to communicate more effectively (and more efficiently, because it will keep matters on track). Again it is a skill to be cultivated, part of the comprehensive overall ability you need as a communicator if you are to use this ability as a skill to further your career.

So far in considering communications, the points have been about communications generally. This is important enough, but there are several aspects, or particular forms of communication, which are especially important to the effectiveness of an individual in an organizational environment, and thus to their career prospects. We turn to these in the next few paragraphs.

You must be able to present formally

There is an old saying which runs: 'The human brain is a wonderful thing. It starts working on the day you are born, goes on and on and never stops until the day you must stand up and speak in public.' You may know the feeling, indeed even the most experienced presenter may experience things like a dry mouth, shaking hands, butterflies in the stomach, all of which can make speaking 'on your feet' a traumatic experience.

Quite recently, a firm approached me as a consultant. They had both a complex organization and a complex pattern of obtaining business which involved formal presentations as one of the key stages. Some of their technical people were poor at this, and I was asked to suggest how they could arrange matters so that the technical people did not have to undertake presentations.

Wrong question – their customers wanted to reassure themselves about the technical viability of their products and services – they wanted to hear what the technical people had to say. The answer then had to be to equip them to tackle the presentational task better.

There are so many circumstances – in almost any organizational or management job – in which the skills of formal presentation are needed, for example:

- Presenting to customers.
- Dealings with suppliers and collaborators.
- Internally (to groups anywhere in the organization hierarchy).
- Negotiations with banks, accountants, shareholders, etc.

There are a hundred and one different ways in which plans, ideas or developments are dependent on how something is put over, and circumstances in which it must be put over on your feet. It is for most, if not all, people *simply not something you can avoid*. There can be only one response from anyone intent on career development: you have to learn to present, and learn to do it well. The influence of this on your ability to get a job done and impress people along the way is just too great. And, should you not need to make presentations in your current job, be very sure you will not need to do so in the next before you reject the need to be able to do it effectively. Many career skills should be seen in this way, considering the future as well as the current need for them.

If you are not currently comfortable with the area of formal presentation, do not despair. It is a skill and can be learnt. (I know. It is an area where I do a great deal of training and I have seen many people over the years amaze themselves with just what they can do, once they know how to go about it – indeed, once I was one such.) What makes it easier? Preparation is the first thing. A clear structure – a beginning, a middle and an end – is important, and there are a variety of tricks of the trade that will assist. A complete run-down on what makes for success is beyond the brief for this book (see my book *Making Successful Presentations* for more detail). But make no mistake: people tend not to say 'What an excellent plan, what a pity it was not better presented', more likely they say 'What a bad presentation, it cannot be much of a plan' – and the same principle is applied to the presenter. Thus good presenters are not only more likely to get approval for whatever is presented, they are in all likelihood going to be seen as a step or two up in terms of overall competence than someone weak in this area. As not everyone can make a good presentation, certainly not without study and practice, this is a real opportunity to shine; certainly those who are not so good tend to respect those who are.

The best way to improve these skills, having investigated them, is practice. It may well be that if you want to add the power of presentation to those skills that will help your career, you should actively seek out opportunities to make some. Providing you think about it, the more you present, the more your technique for doing it will improve. Not only is it useful, there is a great deal of satisfaction to be had from making a presentation that is well executed and well received. So, perhaps you should volunteer for a few things if they are not thrust upon you, to be ready for the day when they matter more – and can help you more.

You must be fluent in written communication

'Writing is easy; all you do is sit staring at a blank sheet of paper until the drops of blood form on your forehead.' This was said (by Gene Fowler) about creative writing, but it might come equally to mind as you contemplate that report you have to submit to the Board in two days' time. The message here is similar to that described regarding formal presentations. Most jobs come with built-in paperwork – some of this is routine administration, some is very important.

Just like presentations, written communication – reports, proposals, even minutes and memos – can have a great deal hanging on them. Decisions that you want to go a particular way may be influenced not only by the quality of the thought, idea or proposal but by how the case for it is made and how it is expressed in writing. Consider a report. Think of one you have had to read. If it is clear, well-structured, descriptive; if it had a clear introduction and a succinct summary that really ties together the key issues, then it makes an impact on you – and it says something about the writer. Any report, on presentation, speaks volumes about the skill, knowledge, expertise, and competence of the writer – and about their clout.

Yours must do the same.

Again, this is a skill that can be developed. In my own case, my career took a path that made certain kinds of writing very important, first with proposals and reports when I first went into consultancy, then later with articles, books and other material.

Not only is there often much hanging on these things, but they have a permanence that, say, a presentation does not. They stay around to haunt you, and bosses are quite capable of producing for discussion at, say, an appraisal meeting, a copy of a report written nine months or more previously. Anyway, in my case I saw the writing on the wall as it were, and concluded it was something I had to work on and improve. I read about it, attended seminars and, most importantly, became much more aware and critical of what I did. My style improved. I do not delude myself that I am the best writer in the world (and the great novel is still on Chapter 1) but I can produce sufficiently workmanlike writing in a number of areas to earn part of my living from it. It is also a skill that you can spend a lifetime fine tuning. So it should be with your business writing – regular work on it will improve it. And an effective and appropriate style will reflect well on you in your current job and in the view taken by others regarding your future.

A last point may provide an added incentive for you to work on your skills in this area. As your writing ability improves, you become able to do it faster. This saves time and is a worthwhile objective in its own right. You have only to look at the quality of much of the paperwork that circulates around many an office to see that prevailing standards often leave something to be desired; so write right and you have another essential skill that can make you stand out.

There are personal business writing jobs too with which effective writing style can directly benefit your career. These include the preparation of CVs and accompanying letters when you are applying for a new job, and internal documents linked to the possibility of promotion or salary review.

Making communication persuasive

With much business communication, it is not enough to be understood; there is a need to persuade. People with whom you must communicate up, down and around the organization (or indeed outside it) are not going to agree with you instantly and automatically just because you communicate well. They have their own point of view and this may include not doing anything, or doing something quite different from what you are suggesting. Selling is, in effect, part of most management jobs. It may not be called that, or even thought of as such, but that is what it is; any other word is perhaps a euphemism.

Now you may feel instinctively that you are not a salesperson and that this is something that you really do not need to be involved in to do your job. You may be right; but how about this: would you like to get your own way more often? Would you like less argument about things? Would you like to be seen more as a leader and initiator, someone who makes things happen rather than who just follows? If the answer to any of these points is affirmative then you need to be able to communicate persuasively. If, in writing the last paragraph, I am doing this it is, in part, because I am putting up a case for your doing so on the basis that it will help *you*. If I just said do it, *I* think it is right, then this is less powerful.

Selling – persuasive communication – demands an approach based on an understanding of the people or person to be persuaded, something that sounds pretty much like common sense, but it is also something where common sense and the various techniques involved need co-ordinating. Thus it needs to be investigated and learned before it can be successfully deployed. However you may do that, there will be many occasions in your career where your progress will benefit from being able to communicate persuasively. Agreed?

This too I would categorize as a career skill; it is one you may plan to investigate further.

You must be an effective negotiator

This is another communication skill with a direct link to effectiveness and career development. Negotiation overlaps with persuasiveness. It is to do not just with whether an idea will be accepted or agreed – that is the job of selling – but *how* agreement will be arranged, what the terms and conditions are to be. Again there are so many applications internally and externally to the organization, and again there is a body of knowledge and techniques skilfully deployed that make it possible. It too is something you may consider worth investigation and practice. The balance of arrangements that negotiation can settle is important to activities all the way up the management hierarchy. If you start as you mean to go on and become adept in this regard it will stand you in good stead. It is yet another skill rightly described as a career skill and worth further study and practice.

Meet with confidence – as a participant

It would be wrong to omit something about meetings from this chapter. Much communication in business is not one-to-one but involves the interactions of groups – the ubiquitous meeting. Sometimes it seems to most of us that we spend far too long in meetings that achieve far too little, a situation that gives rise to descriptions such as: 'The ideal meeting is two – with one absent.' On the other hand, whatever the topic of the meeting, those attending it are on show, especially if representatives of senior management are present. If, when called on to contribute, you are unprepared, tongue tied, incoherent or muddled and indecisive then you not only fail to make whatever point you wanted to make, you are visibly tagged with an 'indecisive' label, or whatever unflattering label seems appropriate to your performance.

So, if you are at a meeting (make sure incidentally that you should be, you do not want to be seen attending what others regard as time-wasting sessions that hamper your productivity; particularly if they prove less than useful), go prepared. Always read the previous minutes, and any notes or papers circulated for discussion, in advance. No matter that others may not – you should. There will be issues that face you that you can only pronounce on with some thought beforehand, and you cannot afford to be caught out for the sake of a moment's homework.

Be careful not to come over as showing off, but remember the key points of effective meeting participation:

- Be prepared.
- Listen.
- Make notes.
- Keep comments succinct and to the point.
- Deal through the Chair and respect the agenda and any meeting formalities.
- Do not be crowded out; if you have a point to make, make it.
- Never resort to unpleasantness or abuse, but be prepared to fight your corner on a rational businesslike basis to make your point.
- Be open-minded and respect others' points of view (though you do not have to agree with them).

Politeness coupled with firmness, assertiveness rather than aggression – all these make for a good meeting, and for good contributions by you. If you can become known as someone who brings common sense, sound thinking and appropriate manner to a meeting, you will get asked to the right ones more often and your performance at them will contribute to your being seen in the right light. Never become unthinking in even a routine meeting – you are always on show and there may well always be something to gain from them.

Meetings also link (or they should do!) to action. You may collect jobs or progress existing projects that enable you to succeed in creating whatever results your job demands.

Meet with confidence – chairing the session

You may well have noticed that however well or badly a meeting goes, its manner is usually a direct reflection of the manner of the chairperson and, if no one is in the Chair, the thing is usually a muddle from beginning to end. You are not going to rise any great distance up most organizations without the ability not only to attend a meeting and perform impressively, but also to chair one.

For the managing director at least, their position and authority will work in their favour to keep things going well in some respects. Saying that reminds me of a meeting many years ago at which I was attempting to get a particular project vetoed and doing so by arguing about its high cost. I was overruled by the managing director (and owner of the company) who said simply, 'It is my money – we will spend it.' You live and learn; but I digress.

Down the line, perhaps having cut your teeth and gained practice on simple departmental meetings, it is perfectly possible to find yourself chairing a meeting where some of those attending are more senior and more experienced than you. So it is an area where, though practice of course helps, you have to make a good start. Therefore, it is another skill worth researching.

Briefly, the key issues for the chairperson are to:

- be prepared (preferably more thoroughly prepared than others attending);
- set and keep to the agenda and keep time (an ability to run to time is especially impressive to others);
- keep control, yet encourage discussion, let people have their say

(drawing in necessary different viewpoints) and comply with any rules;

- be able to field questions, arbitrate in debate and referee in argument;
- see, and deal with, both sides of the case;
- summarize clearly;
- arbitrate where necessary;
- prompt and record decisions and maintain a reasonable consensus.

And more, no doubt. This is another communication skill that will stand you in good stead in a number of fields and circumstances. Resolve to be a good chairperson, acquire the skills to be so and use them fairly, as chairmanship is not about riding roughshod over everyone by sheer weight. Apart from anything else, the roughshod approach will be resented by others. Get things done, but get people feeling they are good decisions sensibly arrived at and that they contributed to the process, and they will be queuing up to attend your meetings!

Lastly, it should be mentioned that meetings skills can, of course, be usefully deployed at job interviews and appraisals; both of which have a direct bearing on successful career development.

Ask questions

There is a danger that we think about communications as being concerned only with how we communicate to pass information or instructions to others. But the ability to thrive and do your job successfully is dependent on knowledge and information, and all you need of this will not be delivered to you on a plate: you have to ask. Sometimes you have to balance this with not becoming a nuisance to those you ask, but otherwise the rule is ask, ask and ask some more. This should become a habit. Its value is cumulative and the result is most often useful, and the impression given positive. Open questions (those that cannot be answered 'Yes' or 'No') tend to work best at getting the most information promptly and easily.

Having asked of course, you must listen – and note – anything you need to retain. Communication is two-way, and abilities in all the specialist areas of communication dealt with here not only highlight the general importance, but also pick methodologies that are prime candidates for career enhancement. It really cannot be stated too strongly: if your communications skills are weak then your career prospects can all too easily be restricted. Even in technical areas where you may feel other specialist skills make up for deficiencies here, they may not be able to be hidden. So give attention to the way in which you communicate and to the method in which you do it. Consider different communications methods specifically.

Select your communication method wisely

Imagine someone telephones you out of the blue. You have not seen them for a while and you invite them for a meal. You are pleased to see them, you lay on the arrangements rather specially and a very good evening results. Then a few days later, you get either a telephone call to say thank you or a specially written note. Which would make the best impression as a 'Thank you'? Most people would probably think that the letter was extra nice, taking more trouble than just lifting the telephone. Certainly, whatever view you take, you should recognize that they do each make different impressions.

So, any medium of communication has its own special effect. And there are a great many ways of communicating: one-to-one, a meeting, a memo or letter, a fax, e-mail, a circular or a note on the company bulletin board. They work in different ways. Take fax, perhaps now a universal form of business communication. It seems to speak immediately, just by its nature, of some urgency (just like cables and telex did), but it can be less formal – people most usually write faxes in what is almost an internal memo style, even to contacts in other companies whom they have never met and to whom they would be much more formal in a letter.

Make a good choice regarding methodology and what you do will be thought appropriate; pick wrong and you are thought hasty, uncaring or unthinking. What is the right way to communicate to someone that they are being fired? Or to a group that one member of the team is now in charge? Or to a senior manager so that he is most likely to give time to think about something? Each case and each person needs thought. Getting it right adds something positive to your image.

The physical nature of the method has a bearing too. E-mail is becoming more and more common. It can be very useful, but it is essentially transient and very easy to wipe out – of both the system and the mind – so it may be less suitable for things where you hope, and feel you need, to encourage someone to keep something. Similarly a fax does not provide such a good quality document for retention (indeed the thermal paper often used allows the message to fade away), so for some things an original letterhead will be better.

For some people, with both the nerve and the clout to carry it off, a unique style can be added to certain communications. I know one manager who sends everything out on a letterhead printed in the colour brown, he has brown ink in his laser printer to match and also signs letters in matching brown ink. The net effect is classy and distinctive rather than pretentious. But add this kind of element with care. Getting the method right can add powerfully to what you communicate, and what you communicate always says a great deal about you.

Join the grapevine

An organization's grapevine, or informal communications network, which was touched on in the chapter on people, may take many forms. In one company in which I worked, it consisted almost entirely of the company tea lady, as she moved round and round the office during the day, so the news – good and bad, accurate and wild rumour – went with her. The tea lady was not intent on doing this so much as primed by those who knew how things worked in this respect – anyone aware of the system could have a word with her when the first tea of the day came round in the morning, and know that everyone in the office that day would get the message by the end of the day.

This may be something of a digression, but it does make a point. Unless you are plugged into the grapevine you may well miss a great deal. Worse, you may put yourself at a disadvantage by not being aware when others are of anything from policy changes to the imminent departure of key members of staff. Of course, you need to be able to read between the lines; not everything the grapevine has to say is true, though even the rumours may have a basis in fact and give you some sort of advance information.

What action does this suggest? First, as I have said, you should work out how the grapevine works and tap into it. Second, you should use it – it is as useful as a channel to pass round what you want to say as it is a source of information. And finally, read, mark and learn from what information it tells you, and use this as part of the image you present of someone well informed, with a finger on the pulse, which can help paint a positive image for you. One caution: if the grapevine is being used politically or maliciously, be very careful; it is one thing to be well informed, it is quite another to be marked down as the instigator of such gossip or one who delights unconstructively in rumour. That does no one's image any good.

Think before you speak

A final point about communication: remember the old saying advocating that we should 'engage the brain before the mouth'. I suspect that many a career has been blighted by some ill-chosen remark or statement and people left with the feeling that it is all too easy to say something in haste and find oneself repenting at leisure. The consequences of any communication may be broad and many. Every time you open your mouth, the image of how people see you is adjusted a little, and you need to think not just of the context of every comment made but on what other results it may have. In part, this is a matter of manner. It is quite possible to disagree without actually saying: 'That's rubbish', though occasionally a – considered – outburst may be the only way to do the job you want. But that is the exception, most often matters in business are dealt with all the better for some consideration, and without going over the top.

Similarly, do not be put on the spot unnecessarily, for example in trying to provide an instant answer to a difficult question. There is rarely a problem in saying: 'I don't know', or 'I would like to think about that', or 'Perhaps I could check'. Certainly there is less chance of a problem if you go down this road than if you charge ahead without thought. If this all seems only like so much common sense, so it is. However, before passing on because you feel common sense is your stock in trade, consider for a moment some of the things that can make charging in more likely: anger, surprise, pressure (at being put on the spot), limited time or pressing deadlines, lack of preparation (perhaps prior to a meeting), dislike of the person or proposition with which you are dealing. All make an ill-considered outburst more likely, all make it less likely that such an outburst will match your considered view or be a well-directed piece of communication.

There are some moments when biting your tongue and a little thought are great career developers. There are more where the form, style and quality of your chosen communication has a very direct effect on your ability to develop your career as you wish.

You may like to keep communication in mind as you read on, especially during the chapter on management, where it is an important factor.

5

Career Skills and Competences

'If you think you can, you can. And if you think you can't, you're right.'

Mary Kay Ash

DIFFERENT JOBS need different skills. I do not doubt that a wondrous grasp of the intricacies of regression analysis will help the statistician, almost as an ability to run fast might help a bank robber. However, after some brief mention of job-specific skills, I want to concentrate here on reviewing something about skills which has common applications in business and in management jobs, as well as more specialist skills. Like some already mentioned, for example in reviewing communications, the skills described here are important in themselves and, in addition, the attitudes to them may well apply to other areas in your particular field. In the future no doubt, changes, currently difficult to predict, will necessitate adding further skills to such a list. Certainly the rate of change is such these days that in an average career of, say, forty years – age 20 through to 60 – many things are simply not going to be the same throughout the time spanned.

The quotation that starts this chapter is all very well. Certainly you have to have confidence to tackle many things, but skills also need to be developed. Let us consider first the technical skills that go with particular jobs.

Getting and staying up to speed

Whatever your job it will demand special skills and the need to keep them up-to-date and add to them as changes occur. If you are in personnel then you need skills in interviewing, appraisal and perhaps in the use of psychometric tests; and much more. You also need to be up-to-date with regard to employment legislation. If you are an accountant then you need to be able to prepare a balance sheet and understand and influence cash flow; and you may also need to keep up-to-date on the ins and outs of ever-changing tax legislation.

Every job has this nature, there are things you need to able to do and those you need to know. This fact demands three approaches:

1. Regular assessment of the immediate 'Can do' factors, not only in terms of looking at what you can (or cannot) do, but the quality or standards to which you can do each. The latter can change as much as the former. For example, the common availability of computer graphics means that much financial information can look ill-considered or incomplete unless illustrated by graphs which make it easier for people to take in the information the figures contain. Standards of presenting the information have changed and there is a need to keep up.
2. Regular consideration of the information you need to do a job well. It is a truism that the modern world is engaged in an information explosion, and organizational life is a major site for it. Most jobs demand constant review of information, information sources and an increasing ability to sort the wheat from the chaff. Having the right information to hand is job- and career-enhancing; being bogged down in a sea of irrelevant information stifles your ability to concentrate on the things that matter most.
3. Regular consideration of likely new skills that you may have to get to grips with.

Many examples come to mind linked to technology and information technology (IT) specifically. The Internet, for example, is something many in business are now involved with and something others are watching with interest. Others may be linked to the development of the organization you are with: global expansion may involve you in things to do with other countries and cultures that were simply not part of the job in the past. Others may link to a variety of other changes in the way an organization works, either positive or negative. Two examples: downsizing may mean your taking on jobs originally done by others whose skills or knowledge was different from your own; or you might find outsourcing puts you in a position of working from home (all or part of your time) where computer communications skills suddenly become important and are something you have to be able to handle personally, on your own away from the office support services. Still more may be involved, specialist skills having to be augmented by more general ones, executive skills (what you do) having to be augmented by those involved in managing other people.

Failure to think about, and act upon, such things (taking such advice as may be necessary along the way) may make you vulnerable, and may – in the longer term – reduce the options you have open to you to make progress either with your current employer, or with others.

In the rest of this chapter we will concentrate on a selection of skills that are, or could be, important across a whole range of jobs. First, one that will not apply to everyone, but is important to some.

Speaking a foreign language

Parlez vous français? Anata wa nibongo o banasemasuka?
This is, in fact, not a universally necessary skill in the way I have just defined above, but it is worth a comment. Language skill has two career benefits. First, it can fit you for particular jobs that you may want to do where fluency in a language is a prerequisite. This clearly links most readily to the international nature of business, to the value of some experience working in a country other than your own, and also to any personal desire you may have to travel or live abroad.

Fluency is important here. Do not over-claim. It will do you no good to be appointed to a job where your level of fluency is simply not up to the requirement; and besides, many recruiters wanting language skills will run a test. If you have a working knowledge, that alone may be useful (and can perhaps be improved), but if a job demands that you are actually bilingual, that is another matter. For example in my own job, certainly in training, a knowledge of a number of languages would be advantageous, but I could only ever conduct training in a language in which I was totally fluent. Nothing else is very much use, and as I am not qualified in this way, my work must be limited to those parts of the world where English is spoken. I have had books translated into more than a dozen languages, but regrettably have no way of checking any of them!

Secondly, even when they are not strictly necessary to a job, language skills impress, and this may just add a little to the way you are perceived, especially if the skill is unusual among your peers. Once, when helping to set up a European office in Brussels for a company, I found myself interviewing secretaries for them. The language requirement was English, Dutch and French. I will never forget the ultimately successful candidate answering the question about how many languages she spoke. 'Six.' (She was Dutch, living in Belgium, married to a Frenchman and with a Norwegian mother and spoke Dutch, French, German, Norwegian, Spanish, Italian and, as she said, 'English, but everyone speaks English, don't they?') This impressed me a great deal; more so when she added very apologetically, 'I am so sorry, but I can only take shorthand in three of them.' Whatever the starting point, whatever you add, languages can be useful.

For those in the earliest stages of their career, and thinking well ahead, this is something that you might link to your decisions about qualifications. For example, it is not uncommon for people to study for a business or management degree overseas. Alternatively there are a number of UK bodies – Middlesex University is one – that offer such courses with some of the time spent in the UK, but part of the course being done while living in another country.

Language ability can help you meet particular personal ambitions and there is also the advantage that languages can be studied in your free time. I know that one of the things I would do differently if I had my time over again is to learn a second language.

Acquire suitable numeracy skills

Mathematics is not everyone's strong suit. But ultimately business is all about profit, and many jobs are involved directly with finance – whether revenue or cost – in one way or another. There are exceptions – non-profit-making organizations, charities, government departments and so on, but, while profit may not be the driving force, finance – or at least staying solvent – usually plays a key role, so a degree of numeracy is important in many jobs. Modern management education makes this a less likely gap than in the past, and even calculators help. Get a programmable one if you need more than basic arithmetic.

For some who are less numerate, the moral may be to avoid jobs with too much involvement in finances; for others, certainly if you are going in the direction of general management, a certain minimal strength here is essential.

There is an apocryphal story told of a management course that illustrates something about this area. On a particular course, one participant could not get anything right in finance and he left the session very much the class dunce. The group planned to meet up in a year's time to see how everyone was faring, and in due course a dinner was scheduled in a smart hotel. The 'dunce' arrived late, but it was clear to all from the Porsche parked in front of the hotel, the suit he wore and a dozen other signs of affluence that he was doing very well for himself. 'I would never have thought it possible', said the course tutor, 'tell us, what are you doing?' 'It wasn't easy', he replied, 'I tried various things, but I finally ended up in the import/export business in Africa. I discovered that I could buy goods on one side of the border for $2 and sell them on the other for $4. It's just amazing how that 2 per cent adds up'. The more numerate reader will recognize that this is not at all how percentages work, and for most of us such a gap in our expertise is unlikely to work out so well.

Be warned. And forewarned is forearmed. It is perfectly possible for most of us to get our heads round the essentials of how corporate finance works; and well worthwhile for most.

Computer literacy

For some, computer literacy is already the norm. Others are currently either struggling or moving closer to some expertise in this area (or, as in my case, struggling to move closer!). It is a process which will never end as the technology moves on inexorably all the time. Whenever this area is commented on, the advice often incorporates the need to become keyboard literate as part of the whole. In time perhaps this may be unnecessary; already the first generation of 'personal communicators' which will accept inputs using a pen – albeit a special one – are available. But it may be a while yet before this – or voice activation – is really at a level where it makes basic keyboard skills obsolete. Incidentally, by having keyboard skills I do not necessarily mean being able to touch type at speed (though this is very useful to many), but I do mean something a good bit more than pecking away slowly and laboriously with two fingers.

The so-called 'IT revolution' (information technology) is having a wide effect on many different aspects of business, not only within an organization, but in terms of communication between organizations and with groups such as suppliers and customers. For example, some salespeople are already carrying and using hand-held terminals to link them to their office; these allow them to record information, check stock and input orders. In some stores computerized cash points not only record what has been sold and adjust stock level records, but in some cases the computer involved can automatically reorder more stock direct from a supplier, computer to computer, with no other action involved (they may also link to personal details about the customer, allowing a store to issue a coupon encouraging trial of one product to a customer who has purchased another brand). One could list a hundred examples, and in a year's time, no doubt, a hundred more.

Most people have to be knowledgeable about what processes can be carried out by computers, many are going to have to work with the various forms of equipment involved and some are going to have to anticipate how all of this will affect their organizations, their people and their commercial prospects. Computers and this kind of technology do not automatically guarantee improvement in every area. There are many things they will not do, some things they will never do, and some where, although technology has revolutionized the way something is done, it does not guarantee achieving the right end result. In some organizations the statement '. . . it is in the computer . . .' has become synonymous with delay or inflexibility. The early computer saying about garbage in and garbage out still applies.

For all that, when push comes to shove, there are few people whose career development is looking ahead to the next millennium who will not benefit from increasing knowledge and operational ability in this exciting field. It is an area to build into your self-assessment, looking at specifics that might help you in your current work and future career. To take a simple example, presentations can be enlivened by slides and good ones can be made straight off screen, and graphics have already been mentioned in the context of communicating financial information clearly. Some private study and practice may be necessary as well as training initiated by organizations (the fact that so many people have a computer at home helps here, though if you do not and need a machine at work you might suggest you have a laptop which can be used at home for both work and training).

Meantime, I continue to set myself modest objectives and remain determined to get the better of the machine on which this book is being written; it has revolutionized my life but there are occasions when it seems to have a mind of its own. Worse to contemplate is that in fact it only does *exactly* as it is told, so any glitches are doubtless my fault. Getting a real grip on whatever forms of technology you have to use, or will have to use in the future, is important, and some thought within career plans about what you may need is certainly worthwhile.

Be assertive

Most if not all organizations are competitive arenas in which to work. It is also a fact of life that excellence in your area of expertise and in your job is not any guarantee of success. In most organizations, there is at least some conflict between departments, activities and individuals. To a considerable degree this is inevitable. In my book *One Stop Marketing* I included a chart, reproduced here in Figure 5.1, which shows how such friction occurs between the main functions of a business.

	Finance	Production	Marketing
Objective	To ensure that the return on capital employed will provide security, growth and yield.	To optimize cost/output relationships.	To maximize profitable sales in the marketplace.
Time period of operation	Largely past – analysing results plus some forecasting.	Largely present – keeping production going, particularly in 3-shift working.	Largely future – because of lead time in reacting to marketplace.
Orientation	Largely inward – concerned with internal results of company.	Largely inward – concerned with factory facilities, personnel.	Largely outward – concerned with customers, distribution and competition.
Attitudes to money	Largely 'debit and credit' – once money spent, it is gone, money not spent is saved.	Largely 'cost-effective' – hence value analysis, value analysis techniques and cost-cutting.	Largely 'return on investment' – money 'invested' in promotion to provide 'return' in sales and profits.
Personality	Often introverted: lengthy training: makes decisions on financially quantifiable grounds.	Usually qualified quantitative discipline; makes decisions on input/output basis.	Often extroverted; often educationally unqualified; has to make some decisions totally qualitatively.

Figure 5.1: How conflict arises between different company functions

It is a natural, perhaps inevitable, process, but make no mistake – its effects are not all bad. Friction and competitiveness can act to keep an organization on its toes, it ensures constant debate and may well have a constructive effect, or be made to have, unless friction becomes too extreme. In any event it is there. The question is, what is the appropriate response to it? The career-minded have, I believe, to adopt an assertive attitude within their work and work environment. There is, it should be noted, all the difference in the world between being assertive and being aggressive. If you are aggressive, and this may well go with – or be seen as going with – being unreasonable, self-seeking, unthinking, selfish and more unflattering descriptions, this is unlikely to do your career much good. Though there are people who bludgeon their way to the top through their sheer aggression, this is not so common, and, many would say, not desirable. Characteristics that are more helpful include being determined and hard-working, having real ambition and pushing for what you want.

Assertiveness is so often necessary in a variety of ways. When you put forward a point of view, a suggestion, or a plan, it must be put over with conviction. If you do not seem to present it with all the courage of your convictions, then why should others feel it is demanding of their attention and consideration?

Assertiveness is at its most powerful when it is considered. That means to say that while sheer assertiveness will add some credibility to a point of view, if that point is not valid, not well thought out or ill-conceived, then there is no great likelihood of it carrying the day. There is no guarantee that a sound argument will carry the day either, but put over energetically – with some assertion (and, if necessary with some power of persuasion) – then it will stand the best chance of acceptance.

This principle must prompt the acquisition of the right habits. Its application would range from how one particular point is emphasized in a conversation, to the preparation of an annual plan or appraisal meeting so that holding back becomes a considered opinion. However, your normal mode of operation and communication, while tailored to the different kinds and levels of people with whom you interact, should always do real justice to the points you wish to make. And if there are any particular reasons to put more clout behind something, it is worth knowing what they are. Maybe you are seen as new, young, inexperienced – or all three. If so you may have to be more assertive than would otherwise be the case; though overdoing it could come over as your being brash rather than making your case stronger.

Perhaps one should consider, for a moment, the questions of gender here also. I remember once seeing a cartoon of a group of people sitting round a boardroom table. There is one woman present, and the chairman is saying: 'That's an excellent idea Miss Smith, I wonder if any of the gentlemen would like to suggest it?' An exaggeration, of course. Of course? Realistically there is an element in many organizations that downgrades their opinion of people and their ideas on the irrational basis of the sex of the individual. Resenting this alone is not likely to change things.

Women have to learn how to compensate for this and this includes knowing when to be more assertive. Many women readers may know the lovely quote attributed to Charlotte Whitton: 'Whatever women do, they must do twice as well as men to be thought half as good . . . luckily, this is not difficult.' Sensitivity is necessary here; protesting too much may become self-defeating, not being sufficiently assertive may condemn you to live below the glass ceiling despite your competence.

Successful careers are built on success. You first have to achieve that success before you can benefit from how it positions you within your organization. Analyse how you come over at present; perhaps you should sometimes consider being just a little more assertive.

No, I will restate that – be more assertive where necessary!

Master decision-making

Decision-making is important in the context of this book in two separate ways. First, the quality of the decisions you make in your job will directly affect your effectiveness and success, and, as is expressed in various ways throughout this book, this in turn affects your career. Second, you have to make decisions throughout your working life about your career, and exactly how you can best do this is worth examining in some detail.

To a degree there are no 'right' answers in business, but there are certainly wrong ones. Experience is a vital factor in guiding us to pick the best alternative, though too much reliance on it can give a false sense of security and may stifle creativity. A procedure that is logical and systematic and that ensures due consideration of the alternatives, whilst not being infallible, will certainly help make more of your decisions, about your work or career, turn out right. Such an approach can be neatly described as consisting of ten steps.

Step 1: Setting objectives

Before any action can be considered, the objectives of the exercise must be set. Unless you know where you are going, you cannot plan how to get there or how to measure your progress. For the objective to be valuable, it must be as specific and as quantitative as possible. Goals such as 'increasing sales', 'improving customer service' and 'reducing costs' are useless, as they provide no basis for measurement. If the aim is to increase sales, it should be specified by how much and within what time period. (Objectives were defined and described on page 27.)

Step 2: Evaluating the objective against other company objectives

When a clear, precise goal has been established, it should be compared with other company aims to ensure compatibility. Failure to do this is common, particularly in large companies. This results in different sections of the organization working towards objectives which in themselves are reasonable but which, when put together, become mutually exclusive: for example, the sales office manager may be trying to maintain business with small accounts, whereas marketing or sales management are planning to service them exclusively via wholesalers.

Step 3: Collecting information

Information can now be collected, from which plans can be developed. It is unwise to start this data collection stage until clear, compatible objectives have been defined, otherwise vast quantities of useless figures will be assembled 'for information' or 'in case we need them'. The hunger for information has been stimulated by the advance of research techniques and the progressive development of the computer. It is a great temptation to any manager to call for information simply because he knows it is available. Mountains of figures may give a sense of security, but information is costly to process and is only useful (and economic) when it contains answers to precise questions which have a direct bearing on the decisions it is possible to take.

Step 4: Analysing the information

It is the objective which will guide the manager towards the questions to be answered and thus the information needed. The lines of analysis to be followed will in turn be indicated by such questions. For example, declining sales in one area of the country, perhaps owing to the larger customers buying from competitors, should not prompt us to ask for 'everything we know about the market'. What we really need is sales in that region broken down by customer type, possibly compared with similar figures for another area. From this analysis, we can proceed progressively through the relevant information, very much more precisely (and probably more quickly and economically) than starting with a dozen different breakdowns that attempt to show 'all about everything'.

Step 5: Developing alternatives

The whole basis of this method of approach is to encourage the manager to think more broadly and creatively about possible solutions to problems. Sometimes, of course, the solution will become obvious from systematic processing of the data. In the majority of instances, however, no clear-cut answers will be found, a number of factors suggest themselves, or the answer lies in a combination of a number of factors.

Step 6: Choosing the 'best' alternative

This is the heart of the decision-making process. It is unlikely that all possible solutions can be implemented; one must be chosen. To help in this choice, consideration should be made of four criteria: cost, time, risk and resources.

The costs of each alternative can be calculated and compared against the objective. Assuming that several approaches appear to be capable of achieving the objective, this might only narrow the choice. So the other yardsticks should also be used. Time taken might be a critical factor, or the element of risk (particularly of failure) or lack of certain resources might rule out other options: e.g. a critical staff situation in an office may preclude certain courses of action. Many decisions involve weighing the pluses and minuses and taking a decision that balances different factors.

The choice of the 'best' alternative then is based on a consideration of all the advantages and disadvantages of all the possible alternatives. It is at this stage that experience can be particularly valuable. Its possible limiting effect will already have been overcome by the systematic search for alternatives.

Having made the choice, at least the manager will be well aware of what they have done in terms of the possible drawbacks of their decision and the discarded alternatives. It will also be easier at some time in the future to look back and assess why such a decision was, in fact, made.

Step 7: Communicating the decision

This applies more to job decisions than to career ones, and it is a step too often omitted. And yet unless all concerned know what is being done, its impact will be lost. For example, it is commonplace to find inside sales staff whose first knowledge of an advertising campaign is gained from customers. The communication must be systematically planned. Information may well have to be passed by different methods and in different forms to different people, in writing, by telephone, meetings, etc. By communicating only necessary information by the most appropriate methods, far better results will be gained than by a blanket memorandum with copies to everybody.

Career decisions do often need communicating (more often discussing) with family and friends who are affected and have their own view to add to the decision-making process.

Step 8: Setting up the control system

Remember that this stage occurs before implementation. This is because in many cases the process of implementing a plan destroys the ability to evaluate it. For example, in a situation where it is believed that inside sales staff lack product knowledge, the decision might be taken to run a training programme. If, at the end of the course, a test is given in which the average score is 90 per cent, it might be concluded that the programme was successful. But if there has been no measurement of what the test score would have been at the beginning of the programme, it can never then be known whether it was successful or not.

Step 9: Implementing the decision

Putting the decision into action should now be easy. It will have been clearly stated what is to be done, towards what objective and why that particular action has been chosen. All concerned will have been informed, and the system of evaluation will have been set. Research has shown that if change is to be implemented, then specific tasks should be allocated to particular people and deadlines laid down for the tasks to be completed. Vague requests for action will often result in failure.

Step 10: Evaluating the decision

Again assuming quantitative objectives, clear decisions and pre-defined control systems, evaluation is simple. The problems of control and evaluation in management are caused by lack of clear yardsticks against which to compare. If the manager simply sets broad qualitative goals of increasing sales 'as much as possible' or improving customer service, they will have the utmost difficulty in evaluating the results. There will usually be no common definition of what constitutes an increase or an improvement.

Figure 5.2 overleaf shows in summary form the decision-making steps, the key points to check at each step and an example of a decision taken by this method, illustrating the process with an example, linked to increasing telephone sales from the office.

Sound, systematic decision-making is a strength in any job. Having run through the details of an approach it is worth noting that one of the greatest failures of decision-making is not making the wrong choice: it is doing nothing. Procrastination will not get things done, allow you to succeed in your job, nor will it assist career development. How many careers, I wonder, have suffered because a person did nothing – leaving things 'for the moment' – when decisive action might have carried them forward?

As George Burns said: 'I would rather be a failure at something I enjoy, than be a success at something I hate.' Certainly to look back and wish not only that things were different, but that you could have decided to make them so, is not a position anyone wants to be in.

A creative approach

Words like 'creativity' and 'innovation' invoke what sound like highly desirable attributes of both organizations and people. They also conjure up typecast images of the creative department in an advertising agency or the innovation inherent as a high-tech company exploits – or creates – the latest developments in their field. Ideas come in all shapes and sizes. They can be revolutionary, or may be better characterized as being evolutionary, developed through the gradual process of change and development by which so much that drives an organization is carried forward. Most jobs involve

Step	Check	Example
1. Setting objectives	Are they specific and quantitative?	To increase direct telephone sales revenue by 10 per cent in next six months compared with same period last year. To increase customers to 500. To hold sales costs at same level as last year.
2. Evaluating the objectives.	Do they conflict with goals?	Production is available, also promotional help.
3. Collecting the information.	Have the questions to be answered been clearly defined?	Need last year's sales broken down by customer, product and telesales operator. Also market research data on potential available and competitive activity.
4. Analysing the information.	Is it known what is being researched for?	Specific questions to be answered include: Can current customers buy more? How many prospects are there? What is current salesforce call rate? What is order:call ratio?
5. Developing alternatives.	Have all possibilities been listed?	(Assuming above work done) (a) Increase call frequency on customers. (b) Increase prospecting rate. (c) Improve selling skills by training.
6. Choosing the alternative.	Have all alternatives been evaluated in terms of cost, time, risk and resources?	(a) Cost increase because need more operations. Delay in recruiting. Risks in taking on more new men. Personnel dept resources involved. Employment legislation considerations. (b) No-cost – can do with existing team. Some time to reorganize. Low risk. Low resource use. (c) Cost of training. Time for training. Experience elsewhere shows training effective therefore risk low. No resources, can use consultants. Choose (c) as likely to be most effective though not cheapest.
7. Communicating the decision.	Have the right people been told the appropriate information by the appropriate methods?	Advise marketing director by memo. Brief inside sales team meeting. Give terms of reference to consultants at meeting.
8. Setting up the control system.	What will be measured, how and when?	Best yardsticks of increased effectiveness are order:call ratio and average order size. Monitor now before action starts.
9. Implementing the decision.	Have specific tasks been allocated with specific timings?	Run training programme. Revise sales targets. Concentrate on lists of customers with further potential.
10. Evaluating the decision.	Has the decision been evaluated against the objectives?	Appraisal of training programme. Actuals *v* targets on monthly basis.

Figure 5.2: Ten-step decision-making

some of this process, certain specialist work areas consist mostly of this and, generally speaking, senior people tend to have need of the highest skills in this area.

It may be sensible in dealing with such broad concepts to define our terms. Simon Majaro, whose book *Managing Ideas for Profit* is probably the best read on this whole topic, does this neatly by saying that creativity is the thinking process that helps us generate ideas, whereas innovation is the practical application of such ideas towards meeting the organization's objectives in a more effective way. Innovation is thus the essence of corporate success, taking ideas and converting them into practical and workable ways forward. This being the case, individuals who have innovative and creative ways of approaching things tend to be favoured in choices affecting who rises through the ranks of an organization. Clearly it follows that if you can develop this side of your abilities this may be something else which favourably affects your career.

Some people faced with these comments abdicate all thoughts of success: 'I am just not a creative person', they say, as if it were something you are born with like brown eyes or perfect pitch. Maybe; but there is another view which says you can work at it. Consider an analogy. When someone writes a novel or a film script, something that in a different context would be regarded as a creative act, they need ideas. But they need other things as well: a process is involved which is to some degree structured. A story needs a beginning, a middle and an end. If it is dramatic, each part will end with a cliffhanger or reversal, with the next section turning things round and taking the plot forward. There is a mass of principles about what makes a character, say, sympathetic and all this goes with the ideas that must be built in to create the whole. Much innovation is not, in fact, creative in the sense of the wonderful new idea just popping ready made into someone's head. It is hard graft, it is the systematic working at something in the right way that produces results. It is inspiration and perspiration.

Perhaps producing results is the key. You may never be sufficiently creative to write a sonata that will still be well thought-of in a hundred years' time, but you may well have to produce results for your organization which cannot be done without some original thinking. This you can work at; after all it is not so much creativity which is the key – it is *creating* – and good ideas do not actually care who has them (a manager of a team has a much greater resource than just herself to help create new ideas).

Creativity abounds. I am still surprised (though it happens often) at how in training I can put a group of people, sometimes who have never even met, into a syndicate and they come up with all sorts of creative ideas. When I ask how, and why this does not, apparently, happen so easily day by day in their own organizations, often the answer is that there is no time. Creativity may well involve people working together, and this may need some organizing. Whatever you are doing, the effort involved can be worthwhile.

Take a broad view

One of the things that differentiates management from direction (though not every director from every manager) is their ability to see – and take – the broad view. Again some will claim that this is an inherent skill, others that it is something that can be developed. By broad I mean both in canvas and in time.

An ability to do this is a characteristic shared by many entrepreneurs, or certainly the more successful of them. An initial idea or premise gives rise to a vision of where that can take them, the kind of organization that can be built on it, the way it will work to create success and what it will bring in terms of rewards. Someone has to handle the details as well, of course, but most jobs benefit from taking the broad view and anyone who can stand back, particularly from immediate concerns or problems, and get things in perspective is likely to increase their effectiveness. Sometimes achieving this only means curbing the natural tendency to 'jump in'. This can show itself in both positive and negative situations. If someone identifies a problem and says, 'What can we do to solve this?' the temptation is to focus hard up-front on the problem and possible solutions. But solutions may come more readily if the problem is seen in context: Why is this occurring? What are we trying to achieve? Similarly with opportunities: ask 'What can we make of this?' The best response may be to consider hard whether making anything of it will fit in with the overall activity, rather than instantly suggesting three or four development possibilities. The same principle of thinking should span activities. General management must always think about finance, resources, people and the market and a dozen external factors, and more, always with the precise combination of factors matching the subject of consideration.

You may have such skills already, or have them in embryo form. If so – cultivate them, consciously take a broad view even of matters within a smaller scale in your own part of an organization; if not start to develop them, particularly if you have a directing role in mind for yourself. And apply exactly the same thinking to your deliberations about career development. Something might look like a jump ahead, but how will it be in five years' time? Where will it have taken you? Similarly with factors other than time, how will an opportunity affect not only your working day, but your long-term prospects, your family, and your way of life?

Holding and using information

There is a saying for every occasion, and one that is most certainly true in the context of business careers is: information is power. At the risk of quoting too much, the other well-known saying that has relevance here was something said by Dr Samuel Johnson: 'We know a subject ourselves, or we know where we can find information upon it.' In other words, what matters is not simply the information you have, but knowing where to find what you do not have. You need your wits about you to make progress in many organizations and, without doubt, one way in which this manifests itself is in the information you can marshal together, and which you can do without hassle or delay. It is often said as a compliment that someone has all the facts at his fingertips. In the remainder of this chapter we look at some factors that help make that possible.

Deciding what you need to know

The first step, if you are actually to have everything that matters at your fingertips, is to decide what you need to know and particularly to decide what is most important and thus must be kept in mind or close at hand. Like it or not, in common with everyone else on the planet, your mind does not have an infinite memory and often it does not have an infallible one (more of this later). Nor do you have unlimited storage in your office, so you must decide what you are going to keep.

There can be no list here that is right for everyone, and what you need will vary depending on your job, your employer and the stage of your career you are at. It may well vary as time goes by on both long- and short-term scales. Some categories may help, however:

- *Policy and guidelines* – some of these you need in mind, the rest nearby; you will not endear yourself to the boss or anyone else if you are constantly checking the policy on routine matter; less so if you apply it incorrectly.

- *Figures* – statistics, sales or productivity figures, ratios, percentages; every business and every department has some that are important.
- *Records* – anything from a contract to a schedule.
- *Personal details* (we picked this up in the section on people).

The trick is not simply to decide the categories that are important to you, but to decide what and how much to keep on different topics and in different files. The computer giant IBM once did a study that showed that only 10 per cent of everything put into a filing system was ever looked at again, and there seems no real reason to feel that other organizations are radically different. So, seemingly you can throw away 90 per cent of all the information you hold on file. Actually the problem is not so simple; first you need to consider *which* is the 10 per cent you need to keep. There is a serious point here. Some people seem to keep much less than others yet always have to hand what is required; it is a habit and way of viewing things which can be developed and it is very useful too – one that you would do well to develop.

Obtain the right information

The information base that you need will not just arrive on your desk as if by magic. A fair amount can go in that invaluable filing system WPB (the waste paper basket). Other information you will need to seek out. One-off things have to be dealt with as they arise, regular things are worth a comment. Get yourself on any:

- internal circulation list;
- supplier mailing lists (catalogues, etc.);
- magazine subscription or circulation lists

that will produce useful information for you.

Consider anything and everything else that will help you keep up-to-date and well informed: directories, yearbooks, association membership lists, information services, and keep a note of apparently one-off sources – both internally and externally – that could be useful again in the future. Much information of this sort may these days be held on CD and accessed via a computer screen; the Internet adds to the possibilities (though can lead to enormous expenditure of time in non-priority 'surfing').

Review all these regularly – it is yet something else that must become a habit. Not only will having good information and knowing where to find out the other things you want help you directly; there is usually no harm in becoming known within an organization as a good source of certain specific (and well-chosen) kinds of information. Carefully used, this can keep you in touch with the right people, but watch out that it does not lead to time wasting.

Do any necessary research

Sometimes the information which may support your cause will not exist in your system or indeed elsewhere internally. You should resolve to augment your information with such research as is necessary to update or complete what you have. Never risk basing a case, perhaps for a project or change of responsibilities, on uncertain data. This means you need a line into probably a number of sources of information. What these may be will depend entirely on the area in which you work and the kind of information you are likely to need. They may include other companies, libraries, institutes or trade and industry bodies – and also helpful individuals. People are usually flattered to be regarded as an expert in their field, so, provided you are an appreciative contact (they are not adverse to the occasional 'Thank you') this is certainly possible to build up.

If you can put yourself in the position where some of this is done on an exchange or favour basis so much the better. It is very useful to be able to lift the phone to a friend or acquaintance and borrow a report, check a figure or whatever may be necessary. A reputation for basing everything you do on hard facts is a good one to cultivate. The trick is to make such information easy, quick and inexpensive to come by; and ensure the accuracy and quality involved is good. If you achieve that, such a network can be a real asset.

File systematically

I used to have a slide, which I used on some training courses, which was a cartoon of a secretary standing at her boss's desk. She is holding some sheets of paper and saying: 'Do you want these again, or shall I file them?' Fair comment. Some filing systems are the office equivalent of the black hole. So decide how you are going to keep things and file systematically.

Some things will go in files. A series of A–Z sections (projects, people – whatever you deal with) is better than one large system. A secretary may file things, and she may help work out the system, but you should decide where things go. This is likely to be more consistent, and it is annoying to spend time checking whether the papers on a particular deal are filed under Z (for the organization's name), C (for Cost saving project), N (for Negotiations) or T (for 'Thank goodness that's over'!). The clearer things are to everyone, not just you, the better. As my secretary of the time once said to me: 'When you are on the other side of the world and need something, just how am I supposed to know what is in a file labelled "Possibly"?' Yet most of us are guilty of this kind of labelling.

Follow all the rules of filing:

- Do not duplicate information needlessly (incidentally this can include deciding that if a perfect and accessible record of something you only need occasionally is kept in, say, the Accounts department then you will not keep a complete duplicate); file regularly.
- Run a consistent system.
- Clean it out regularly (perhaps by using a destroy date).

Do everything in fact to keep yourself straight in this respect.

Next note that information storage is involving less and less paper. You may well need to bring such thinking to bear on the way you use a desktop computer, a laptop computer, microfiche storage, personal organizer and – in the future – who knows what. All devices must be used appropriately. It is one thing, to take a simple example, to store all the telephone numbers you use in an electronic gadget – it may be more convenient or teach you something about the gadgetry involved, but it could be a waste of time. After all, the ubiquitous notebook still works very well; and it has no battery to run down and delete its every entry.

This is another area that is not simply for your convenience but which has an effect on others. I remember well the accountant in one company for which I worked. The accuracy of his filing was uncanny, and apparently anything, however obscure or from however long ago was lifted off the shelf in seconds. It was impressive and he was held in higher esteem than would have been the case without this characteristic. It also kept him much better connected around the firm than might otherwise have been the case, as people beat a path to his door because he was such a good source of information.

Finally, 'Start as you mean to go on' is good advice here. It is always worth taking a moment to set systems up as you want them rather than wasting time for evermore with a system that never quite performs with the efficiency you would wish.

Other competences have already been mentioned in discussing communications (which encompasses some important ones), more will be reviewed before we end (particularly in the context of management); for the moment we turn to how to strengthen or add to them through training and the effect that can have on a developing career.

6 / Training and Development

> 'Change is not made without inconvenience, even from worse to better.'
>
> *Richard Hooker*

THOUGH SOME WHO leave school aged fifteen without a qualification to their name become successful, in the last few years more and more of those in business have become better and better qualified. In addition, a more diverse range of qualifications is now in evidence. Using the word in its widest sense, such qualifications range from degrees to attendance on a short course, and cover technical matters of all sorts as well as the techniques of business and management overall.

A degree, or more specifically a business degree, is regarded as the basic by many organizations. But more may be necessary – and usually any ongoing education in business should have a practical bias. It was once said, probably by someone not so qualified, that the perfect business enterprise was to set up a trading enterprise that purchased MBAs for what they were worth and sold them for what they thought they were worth! The point being that the arrogance of the MBAs would ensure a significant profit. By and large such qualifications are also practical these days, but whatever the prime qualification it should be a beginning and not an end.

Here we look at a number of career-building factors to do with ongoing development of various kinds.

Assess your development needs

To say you are actively developing your career in terms of training and everything that word implies, does not mean grabbing at every opportunity to, say, attend a course, regardless of any consideration except that it is possible. You need to consider what development is necessary (which in job terms is what will happen at many organization appraisal meetings). It is worth thinking this through in a systematic way and, of course, doing so honestly. Otherwise, your career will certainly suffer if you deceive yourself and ignore gaps in your knowledge or skills that it is in fact necessary to fill.

First, you should remember that development can only do three things:

- Improve your knowledge.
- Develop your skills.
- Change your attitudes.

With that in mind, consider the thinking involved in an ongoing systematic review, described here as a ten-step process:

1. *Identify the requirements of your current job in terms of knowledge, skills and attitudes* – you need to be honest about this and think broadly about it (and it is clearly easier if you have a clear job description).
2. *Identify your own current level of such knowledge, skills and attitudes* – look at how well you can perform in the job now.
3. *Identify any additional factors indicated as necessary in future because of likely or planned changes* – in today's dynamic business climate there are always likely to be some of these.
4. *Consider and add any additional aspects that your own longer-term career plan demands* – this can look as far ahead as you wish, but realistically should concentrate primarily on the short/medium term.
5. *Set priorities* – note what needs to be done: there may well be more than it is realistic to change very quickly and you then need to set clear priorities to help you make progress.
6. *Set clear objectives* – always be absolutely clear what you are trying to do and why.
7. *Consider the timing* – in other words, when any development can take place, and this no doubt in a busy life means one thing at a time and perhaps at a slower pace than you would ideally like.
8. *Implement* – do whatever is necessary to complete the development involved. This could be very simple: you doing something that you can control. Or it could involve discussion and debate with others to get agreement about the need and the necessary time and money.
9. *Evaluate* – this is an important one. Many people forget to really think through how useful and relevant something is like

attending a course, when a little review can ensure a much better link to the real job and future tasks.

10. *Assess against the job/career factors* – as well as evaluating general usefulness of anything done, you need to match its effect with both current tasks and future career plans to see how well it helps with your specific work and plans.

Then you are back to the beginning again. The process is a continuous cycle, something where regular review is necessary, if not month by month then certainly year by year. Next you need to relate this to a plan (with some intentions noted on paper) and then think about the actions that are implied to see it through. We turn to these next.

Have a self-development plan

In today's dynamic world, development must be a continuous process. As has already been said, there will be new skills you need to acquire during your career and perennial skills to be kept up to date. These may be technical or job process related. If you are with an organization that has a sound development policy, the thinking needed here may well be prompted by what action is forthcoming from such activity. If not, or if what is done is, in your view and for your needs, inadequate, then you will need to initiate what happens here. You need a plan. This need not be something cast in tablets of stone that stretches into the future and is unchangeable, but a rolling plan, something that sets out your immediate actions or intentions clearly and gives an outline intention for the longer term. The detail of this will have to change as events unfold, and you must adjust to changing circumstances and needs, both as they affect your current job and your vision of future ones. Some such changes are fairly long term. In my own case, learning to type did not feature on my development plan for many years; then the increased amount of written work I did coincided with the lower cost and easier availability of computers and word processing. It made sense to learn, so it went on the plan. Now the objective is to do it more accurately and faster!

Other changes may be more rapid, and still affect your development intentions. A move to an overseas office, perhaps, or the organization setting up an overseas subsidiary might prompt thoughts about language skills. Other changes such as entering a new product or market area may also give rise to new areas of knowledge and expertise which need to be tackled. There are several options:

- The organization may suggest something (e.g. attendance on a course).
- You may want to suggest something to them.
- You, or they, may want to amend or adapt an original suggestion.
- You may conclude that whatever the company does, you will only meet your own personal objectives by doing some work in your own time.

The permutations are, of course, many. The key thing initially is that you devote a little time regularly to considering what you feel would help. This means looking at immediate job advantages as well as long-term career ones (after all, the company will be more inclined to spend money on things that have a reasonably short-term impact for them, while you may want to look further ahead) and keeping your personal plan – which should be in writing – up to date.

There is an important link here with any company appraisal scheme in which you find yourself taking part – many organizations have such schemes. Some consist of just an informal annual meeting, others are more formal and more regular. Such schemes, if they are good, are very much to be commended (and are returned to later). Whatever kind of scheme there is, it is likely that you will find it consists, in part, of a review of development needs. This is the moment to link your personal plan with that of the organization for which you work. With the support and approval of your immediate boss, you will probably find you can do more that will benefit your current job and the tasks it entails, and get more benefit for what will help you in the longer term.

Just as you need a career plan, you need a development plan. All business literature commends, indeed advocates, planning. This is not just because it is a formality that the academic texts insist on: it really works. If you take a moment to keep your thoughts straight about this area, you will be more able to action more of what you want and will be better able to take advantage of circumstances.

A final point on planning: some development is interesting, some may even be fun; that is all well and good, but it does not mean it *all* will be. Some of the most useful developmental activities may be a very great chore. For example, to return to my earlier example, the typing course I went on was no fun at all; it was tiring, boring and definitely a chore. But it was very useful. My typing may not be peRfikT but it is good enough to have changed my work pattern in useful and productive ways.

You may not know what skills or knowledge will change your own work pattern in future – but beware of putting off acquiring new skills because the process of doing so is a chore.

Read a business book – regularly

As I make my living, in part, by writing, this may seem like a plug, but reading is certainly among the simplest forms of development, and a good deal can be learnt from it. It takes some time, but it is low cost and is also something that you can allocate to certain moments when perhaps time would otherwise be wasted. Such time includes travelling – I know of more than one salesman who always carries a business book to read in those, sometimes long, moments he regularly spends in his customers' reception areas. The amount of travelling done on business makes this an option for many people in all sorts of jobs.

The first rule is to make it a habit. Always have such a book on the go (even if it takes you a while to get to the end) and keep watching for what is current in book shops, by reading the reviews in the press and getting yourself added to publishers' mailing lists, or to those of distributors.

There are two kinds of book to concentrate on. The first consists of those titles that link directly to your development need, like *'How to do this or that'*. These may reflect immediate needs or something you wish to develop further ahead. Remember it may be useful to approach things in different ways – the constructive repetition involved will help you take in the message, so it is worth reading more than one title on certain topics. There are also other options such as audio book summaries which you can listen to in the car.

The second category are those books that are sufficiently popular (and useful – though the two do not always go together!) that you need to be seen to be up to date with them. I will resist mentioning recent titles (and thus having to predict what will last), but such a book is something like the classic bestseller *In Search of Excellence* (Thomas J. Peters and Robert H. Waterman). This, which reviewed those factors that seemed to be common amongst successful companies, was certainly interesting and some of its phraseology, e.g. the concept of 'sticking to the knitting' (concentrating on key issues with a direct influence on results) soon became regularly used in conversation around many companies. There is a danger in such circumstances that you will be perceived as not up to date if you are not familiar with such titles, though this should not be taken to extremes; if all your conversation becomes hung around quotes from such books, people may think you do not have an original thought in your head.

Doing this may seem a small point, but applied conscientiously its effect may be considerable. A book every quarter, for instance, is still quite an input of information over, say, five years of your career. Six a year is better still. And you can apply the same principle to management and trade journals, picking those that are most useful to you and perhaps using abstracting services to minimize reading time.

Course attendance

Courses, seminars, workshops – whatever word you use, attendance on these events can be very beneficial. And in the long run a couple of days spent on such an event is not too high a price to pay compared to what may be gained from them. Some employers will regularly give you the opportunity to attend both external courses or those set up and run in-house for their own personnel; if not, you may want to prompt them. If you are making such suggestions, particularly to attend outside events, remember you must put your case persuasively. Just ask to attend and some of the thoughts that come to mind will be negative: 'They want my job', 'Once they have extended their skills a little more they will be likely to leave the organization'. Tell them what *they* will get from your attending, and emphasize any short-term advantages. Explain what more you will be able to do for them and for the organization; will you be more effective, more productive, able to save or make money?

Choose events carefully. If you make wild suggestions, something that clearly only benefits you in the long term, or ask to attend something every week, you are unlikely to get agreement. Make practical suggestions and get approval and you perhaps create the right kind of precedent and habit. I remember once battling for three years for the budget and time to attend a conference in the United States. Once I had been and it proved useful, then it rapidly moved to being a regular event. Certainly the most important consideration is always the topic and the content, but realistically there are other things to think about: who is organizing it, speaking at it, and attending it? The style of events is important also; I am not alone for example in finding some of the best-known 'gurus' disappointing in the flesh. You may want something with an international flavour or with specific relevance to your own industry or activity.

One single new idea, or even one single existing idea confirmed with sufficient weight to prompt you into action in some particular area, is all that is necessary to make this process worthwhile, and at best there is a great deal more to be gained by it. So much so that we go on to investigate some specific aspects of course attendance.

Conduct yourself suitably at courses

It is said that you only get out of something what you put in. Certainly this is true of course attendance. First, once attendance is fixed, you should think through what you want to get from it. This will help both you and the course tutor – I know my heart sinks if I ask people on seminars which I conduct why they are present and their only answer amounts to 'I was told to be here'. Never go to a seminar without a written note of your objectives and any specific questions you want to obtain comments on. Most lecturers are happy to get a note of questions in advance, but in my experience this is rarely done.

Thereafter you need to think about how you will behave on the day. If the programme is internal, you may know all the other participants and the whole tenor of the event may be informal. If it is external, it can be a little more daunting to arrive in a room full of participants, none of whom you know. Everyone is in the same situation, however, and the informal contacts and the comments and shared experience of your fellow participants may be an important part of your attendance.

Figure 6.1 sets out the suggestions I often issue to course participants and makes, I think, some useful points about being open-minded and adopting an approach which is constructive when you are a course participant.

In view of the time and cost of attending such events, it is a great pity to walk away at the end with some key question still unanswered.

So, it is important to adopt the right approach. A course may last a week or two, longer, or just a day or two. In every case, however, time goes all too quickly and it is easy to leave and then wish you

NOTES FOR DELEGATES

1. This manual contains all the basic details of this training programme. Further papers will be distributed during the course so that a complete record will be available by the last session.

2. This is *your* seminar, and represents a chance to say what you think – so please do say it. Everyone will learn from your comments and the discussion which follows.

3. *Exchange of experience* is as valuable as the formal lectures – please listen to what others say and try to understand their point of view.

4. In discussion *support your views with facts,* examples or comparisons and stick to the point.

5. *Keep questions and comments brief* – do not monopolize the proceedings, but let others have a say so that several views are made known.

6. Make points as they arise, but remember that *participation is an attitude.* It includes listening as well as speaking. However, never be afraid to disagree in a constructive way, as issues arise.

7. *Make notes as the meeting progresses.* There is notepaper in the binder for this. It can be useful to note separately three key ideas from each session that you can implement without delay. This manual can remain as a permanent record, but only you can make sure that ideas are implemented and the catalytic effect of this programme is not lost.

8. *A meeting with colleagues or staff* on your return to your company can be valuable and ensure information or instructions can be passed on promptly with a view to action.

9. It will be helpful to everyone present if you will:

   (a) *wear your lapel badge* throughout the seminar;

   (b) *adhere to the timetable* so that no time is wasted.

10. Please be *sceptical* about your own operations as well as of the course. Only by questioning present standards can progress be achieved.

Figure 6.1: Rules for participants

had asked something else. Try not to worry about what people will think. Sometimes you may feel others are all ahead of you in understanding. Often they are not, and the question postponed, because it seemed obvious and likely to make you appear stupid, actually – once asked – proves to be a common question which leads into very useful discussion for all.

Maximize course attendance benefits

The most important thing about any course you may attend is what happens after it is finished. Courses may be interesting, they may even be fun, but what really matters ultimately is the action they prompt. So even more important than the notes you make before attending is the action plan you make afterwards.

Such a plan has to start at once when you are back at your desk. It is inevitable for most people that if you are away for even a couple of days at a short course, you are going to have more in the in-tray on your desk afterwards than if you had not attended. Yet the moment to start any action resulting from the course is the following day. Nothing later will do, the likelihood is that you will get involved in catching up and everything will be put on one side and forgotten.

So whatever else you do, take ten minutes on the day after attendance to list – in writing – the areas of action you noted during the programme. This need not be lengthy; it might be six words on a notepad and still be very useful. At least get things down on your 'To do' list, whether they are things to think about, to review further or to take action on; whether they represent things you can implement alone, or things you will need support or permission for and must raise at the next appropriate meeting. If you do this much and then approach them systematically, and with an eye on the priorities, something useful is more likely to happen. If you miss this stage, the danger is not that you will do less, but that you will do nothing. Things you want to action may seem more logical to a boss whose permission is sought in the immediate period after money has been spent on your attending something developmental.

So, follow up your notes, do not just make good intentions but also firm action plans. Consider too:

- reviewing and keeping safe any course notes that were useful;
- having a de-briefing session with your boss, the training manager or whoever sent you. If they are convinced it was useful, then future requests may be that much easier to make and be agreed to. When to do this is worth considering. There cannot be much implemented action to report immediately after attendance, but your recall of the detail will be greater. Later on, you can review what you have done as a result more realistically. Thus two meetings may be worth while. If your company asks you to complete an appraisal form about the course attended, always do so

thoroughly and on time, they are useful in a large organization to the process of deciding what training is used in the future. Keep a copy, especially if you have to complete two, one to record an immediate reaction and one, perhaps some months later, to give a more considered view. Not doing this may be seen as indicating you have no interest in training, and this may affect what you are offered in future.

Also, from a career record point of view, file away details of the course (and maybe the certificate of attendance) and add it to a list you can keep with your CV. This is worthwhile as the memory fails quickly. Five years on, when someone asks what you know about something, it may be useful to look up exactly when you attended a course on the topic and what it covered.

Just attending a developmental event is nearly always of some use – if it is a well-chosen and practical one it may be very useful; and if you go into the process with the right attitude and take the right action before, during and after the event, you will maximize the benefit that comes from it. This is useful in the long and short term – to job and career.

Take a developmental sabbatical

By this I mean taking time away from work to do some additional and longer course. A post-graduate business diploma may be both a useful qualification to add to your CV and you may learn a great deal in doing it. Other kinds of training, even just time spent recharging the batteries and doing something completely different from your job (say working for a charity or travelling) may also be useful. But, whatever you contemplate, the pursuing of it may be sufficiently disruptive to a career to cause pause for very careful thought.

Consider how you could go about this. Either your employer must sponsor you, accept you will be away for six months, a year or more, and perhaps finance this, at least in part; or you are going to have to stop work for a while and sustain yourself during the time such a course takes. The first is a major expense for the employer, one that they will need some persuading to undertake and are realistically unlikely to do so unless they view your potential value to them very highly; do not ask for such an arrangement lightly or on your first day at work! Some may do no more than promise to consider rehiring you after the course is finished. The latter, of course, is expensive and difficult for you.

The other factor to consider is the time taken. You must balance how your career might progress in, say, a year with your current job and employer against what might be possible after taking a year out to attend additional education. But people certainly do it, and I have known those who made considerable sacrifices to save the necessary money and organize family affairs so that they could do a particular course. Usually the choice of institution attended is a prestigious one in order to maximize the career-enhancing effect of the new qualification in due course. Sometimes this means somewhere overseas, and this may be especially worthwhile for some, though it clearly increases the cost.

A final point here: age is no real barrier. I have known people take an additional year (more in some cases) in their twenties or thirties. Conversely, I have even heard of some who took early retirement, undertook extensive new training and then set out to start a new career in a new field. Whether anything like this is worth considering depends on the qualifications you already have, what you want to do next from a work point of view, the sheer ability to organize job, family and more to make it possible – and your own commitment to seeing it through; it is not for everyone, so proceed carefully.

Go on learning – at a distance

Change, including technological change, affects almost everything in our lives; including education and training. One comparatively recent development in this area is the advent of what is called 'distance learning'. This is a rather imprecise term that covers a range of rather different things, but the principle in all cases is similar – that of receiving some kind of formal training (including education resulting in a qualification) by working alone, linked to – but not actually attending (or not more than occasionally) – the establishment providing the tuition. In a sense it is a sophisticated modern version of what used to be called correspondence courses.

The options are many and varied, and allow you to study part time while continuing to work full time and develop your career on the job front. You can undertake anything from an MBA or an NVQ to a short course covering some individual skill area. The form of the course will include conventional study, with things to read, but may also involve a series of other methodologies: videos, exercises, programmed learning and, in the best formats, the ability to complete projects and papers that are sent away and then receive individual critique and comment to help you through the whole exercise. Some courses do involve some group activity, and weekend sessions are sometimes used to fit this aspect in without making it impossible for those working full time to attend.

The area is worthy of some investigation for anyone wishing to extend their learning. But, a word of caution – because of the profusion of material that has become available, there is, amongst excellent material and schemes, some that is frankly not so good. A good deal of work is involved in any lengthy distance learning course so it is worth selecting what you do carefully, and also reviewing the considerable differences in costs that occur.

Like anything you may do to bolster your learning, there is a perception involved. The course may be good, and you may learn something that will benefit your career. In addition, the fact of your doing it, and the commitment clearly implied, makes a point to people and this too may count positively on your overall record. There are some institutions and providers that are more likely to make this kind of impact than others. So the total basis of choice must allow for all these factors.

Take on new things

A last point here which is a little different in nature, but still logically comes under the development heading. Make a point of taking on new things. Experience and the range of your competence are both things that must be kept moving, like sharks which must keep swimming or sink. There is a temptation in many jobs to stick with the areas of work which are 'safe', by which I mean where you do not have to stretch and where you are sure of what you can do. Doing this is almost always a mistake. If you spread your learning too wide you may end up with some expertise across too broad a front rather than a real strength in particular areas. An ongoing objective to broaden your range of skills, expertise and experience is likely to be helpful to you in the long run. A new job – your next job – will, if it represents a worthwhile move, almost certainly contain new challenges. If you have not had any recently, this may come as a bit of a shock to the system; and being, as it were, out of practice may prevent you from getting off to the good start you want.

As the US novelist Henry James said, 'experience is never limited, and it is never complete', not only is the potential for broadening yourself vast, so are the possibilities of something added to your range of abilities to help make a positive career development or change possible.

Developmental opportunities are all around you. The need is recognized by some companies, and their resource centres have a focus on long-term development (even if that involves a future in which someone no longer works for them). Whether you take an hour to attend a training film – or work through something similar on CD-rom in interactive form at your desk – or study in the evenings for a year, all such inputs can, when well chosen, stand you in good stead for the future.

You never know what the future holds and, at the risk of sounding very old, it is an easy mistake among the young to rule out possibilities on the grounds of some inherent prescience. I know from my own experience that skills that have helped me more recently in my career formed no part of my expertise early on and, with hindsight, I do not think I predicted as well as I would have liked what would be useful in this sort of way. So, next time something new is on offer, something that will stretch your powers and even where the outcome is somewhat more certain, think very carefully before you decide to avoid it or say 'No'. You could be taking on something that will kick-start your career into its next move forward.

7 Achievement Versus Activity

'Genius does what it must, and talent does what it can.'
Edward Bulwer-Lytton

THERE IS A SAYING that, in business, one must never confuse activity with achievement. It is true. Never deceive yourself that being busy, applying yourself, putting in the hours or whatever, ultimately scores many points. It may not score any. What is noticed is results. When it is said, within a particular organization, that promotion is 'on merit', it means, putting it bluntly, that you will only make progress if you succeed in your current role. So things that improve your current and immediate effectiveness will, in turn, help your career. Career success is dependent, to a large degree, on your expertise in your chosen role. In this chapter we review a mix of common factors that will help everyone.

Recognize and accept Pareto's Law

This principle, named after the famous Italian economist Vilfredo Pareto, is more popularly known as the 80/20 rule. It has various applications in business and here can be most usefully related to the fact that only 20 per cent of what you do will have a real effect on results – influencing 80 per cent of what you achieve. It is the root cause of the fact that some people in business always seem to complete those things that bring them recognition, and others always seem to be hidden behind a never-reducing pending tray. This principle is true of time and effort.

Figure 7.1 overleaf illustrates the point graphically.

The effect of this ratio may sound harsh, after all you are no doubt always busy and everything seems important at the time, but the principle is a strong one. While the figures will not be exactly 80/20, something close to the ratio will be the case; the rule is true. It means 80 per cent of your time is taken up with activity which,

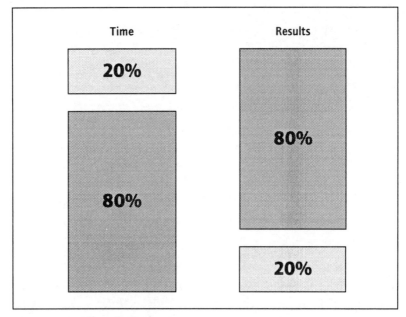

Figure 7.1: Results and Pareto's Law

however much it must be done, is less than key. What is more, the ratio can be applied to specific areas of work as well: for example 20 per cent of time spent in meetings produces 80 per cent of the decisions (and very probably 20 per cent of the content in this book will be more relevant and useful to you than the rest). Realistically every job includes numbers of essential activities, those that are key to achieving what the job demands, as well as a profusion of minor activities which, though they have to be done, do not contribute to success to the same degree.

Recognizing this is itself a significant step to ensuring that the 20 per cent is given due consideration; and that, in turn, should prompt you to have a very serious look at time management (discussed next), for both can have a direct effect on your effectiveness and therefore on your being seen to achieve objectives.

Managing your time effectively

In whatever area you work, you will have noticed that some people seem to manage their time better than others. Like so much else, this does not just happen. And it is without doubt one of *the* key factors governing success in work and in career. If two people have the same skills and, all other things being equal (which they are not, of course, but the point remains), one manages their time better than the other, then the former may well both achieve more and make better progress. Managing your time effectively not only allows you to be more productive, do more and be able to concentrate on the key tasks as necessitated by Pareto's Law, but the results you produce – and the deadlines you hit as a result – will most likely be noticed.

Good time management labels you as an achiever. The reverse, even a small lapse from good organization like always being late for appointments, can label you as wholly inefficient. Can you afford to have your reputation diluted in this way?

Time management is perhaps the classic area of good intentions. Everyone says they are going to manage their time well. Some buy expensive time management systems and electronic gubbins designed to contain – and organize – their life. But if I had the price of a beer for everyone who has said that and not, if they are honest, done anything about it, then I could have retired instead of writing this book! No system can manage your time for you – time management is about self-management and therefore about self-discipline. This means it is a habit and, as such, while it may take effort to acquire, the whole process does become easier once you have made a commitment and done some ground work. What are the key disciplines? Let us consider, briefly, the main factors.

First, you must plan to plan. You need a system, and it can be a loose-leaf diary or notebook rather than a generic system (it can, of course, be electronic if you prefer), that allows you to note what you have on the go, to prioritize it and to progress the various tasks and projects for which you are responsible. Sensibly it will link to, or include, a diary. I have yet to meet anyone who can truly hold all that is necessary in their memory, though some claim to do so; some record is surely always necessary in writing.

The second rule is to update your plan regularly. How long this takes will depend on the job you do. For the majority of people no more than five minutes will be necessary each day. When you do this is a matter of personal preference – first thing in the morning or as you pack up for the day are times favoured by many.

So far so good – and now the next step. You simply have to do what the plan says! This, of course, is where it tends to become difficult. So many things conspire to stop you and it is here that the classic timewasters need controlling: too much time in

unproductive meetings, too many interruptions, too much repetitive administration or time spent hanging on the telephone. You
can – must – work at all of these; the detail matters, but two things
especially need watching. You can control both:

- putting off what you dislike or find difficult – it is often constantly thinking about a task, shuffling papers, but coming to no
  conclusion or action that wastes so much time;
- spending too much time on the things you like, and this often
  means the things you believe no one else is able to do as well as
  you. This is often the worse of the two problems.

If you have ever attended a short time-management course (by
definition good ones will surely be short) you will certainly have
been encouraged to keep a time log. It is always a sobering exercise;
try it for a couple of weeks and, if you complete it honestly, you will
soon see where time goes. Almost always there are surprises, some
things take up very much more time than you think. If you know
how you work, and what happens to your time, you can work at the
details that will make you more productive.

In a sense, it really is true to say 'That's all there is to it.' Time
management may be a struggle to get organized, but the principles
are, for the most part, common sense. The details matter, and small
savings of time, provided time saved is spent on the right things,
mount up and make a useful difference. Two final points: do not
think that because much of your job is unplannable (perhaps
because it is reactive, like the manager of a customer service department who must take customer calls and respond at once, but also
has longer-term tasks to plan out and fit in) you cannot manage it.
You must plan the non-reactive time, and the less you have of it the
more important it is to utilize it effectively.

And, secondly, consider the old maxim that there is never time to
do something properly but always has to be time to do something
again. Regularly you will find that to sort something out may take
half an hour or an hour instead of ten minutes. The temptation is to
get it done and out of the way, rather than pause and take longer.
Take that time once, however, and you may save five minutes every
day in future. That may not sound much, but given the average
number of working days in the year you save around twenty hours;
maybe every year thereafter (and I know I could use an extra two or
three days this year!).

This is a most important area. Unless you get to grips with it you will be at a serious disadvantage *vis à vis* those who do; and thriving in a career is a competitive business. Become a master of your time and you become able to be more effective, both your results and the way you are seen will improve and this is one more help to an advancing career.

Never forget commitments

This next point links closely with time management. In my first job, I was hired as what was euphemistically called a management trainee, more realistically I was a glorified office boy (I escaped into the sales side of the company). I worked for a boss who was the best kind of mentor and from whom I learnt a great deal. Early on, I became convinced he had an infallible memory or used something akin to magic. He *never* seemed to forget anything. He would ask me to do something: 'Have a think about it and we will discuss it at the end of the month', he would say. And come the day if I was not at his office door with it at 9 a.m., the phone on my desk would ring and he would say, 'Now, what about the discussion we planned . . .' He would do this with a couple of dozen people all around the office, registering many, many points with each and doing so in both directions. In other words, if he told you he would let you have something, or would do something – whatever – he would do it; and on the rare occasions where something prevented it, he would forewarn you of it.

This way of working is a good characteristic to find in a boss and it is an equally good one to display to a boss. Reliability is approved, it is efficient – knowing that something will be as planned may be important – and it keeps the majority of contacts you have with more senior managers positive. You do not want their automatic recall of you to be only of the endless occasions on which they have had to chase you for something, but which they regard as having been unnecessary.

My boss at that time owed none of his reputation in this area to magic. He simply had a good system. He had a page in a loose-leaf diary for each person who worked for him, and kept a record of projects large and small linked to his diary. It worked well, and if you build up the reputation of always honouring commitments, whichever way round, that will work well for you.

Always hit deadlines

Although deadlines are a kind of commitment, timing is worth a word in its own right. You do not just need to remember and do *what* the commitment entails but do it *by when* it was arranged. It is said there was never a deadline in history that was not negotiable. This may be true and there is certainly no merit in being pushed into agreeing to a deadline that you cannot possibly meet. It may need negotiation, or at least discussion, to agree something that is possible and will satisfy both parties. Once set, however, a deadline – your deadline – takes on another characteristic: it becomes irrevocable. It can do your reputation nothing but good to be known as someone who delivers on time – not just the major projects and not just when senior people are involved, but everything. Once you have said, 'I'll make sure you have it on Friday week' or something similar, everyone should *know* it will be there.

Always think through any task before agreeing to any particular timing. The more complex the task, the more important this is. Something may appear straightforward, but it is only when you reach stage four perhaps that complications set in, so this kind of realism needs to be built into your estimate of how long it will take – fitting it in, no doubt, amongst the other things you have on your plate. Sometimes in organizations, there is a confusing incidence of what might be called 'deadline abuse'. That is, someone wants something on, let us say, 31 May, so they build in a safety factor and say they need it by 25 May. But people know this is what happens, so it is accepted with the thought that there is always a week or so built in, and that the 2 or 3 June will do. If more people are involved then this scenario rapidly gets much more complicated and the only thing you can be sure of is that as things get passed along and amended on the way there will be a muddle. Deadlines should be honestly stated and then dealt with accordingly.

Treat deadlines with care and you will help your colleagues and others who are dependent on them being hit, and that in turn will help you.

Incidentally, exactly the same principle of reliability and accuracy is useful in the same kind of way in other areas. If you are asked to make a twenty-minute presentation to the Board – sit down after nineteen minutes. If you are asked to 'keep the report down to ten pages or less' – do so. People notice, and they appreciate it.

Decide the right priorities

First things first, it is said. This is a reminder of another area which may be viewed as part of time management, the simple matter of setting priorities. 'Simple' may seem the wrong choice of word and, of course, priority setting is not necessarily easy. But it is a simple fact of life that you can only work on one task at a time. First you do one thing and then you do another, and another. Sometimes you have to pause to tackle something else – this may be an interruption like a telephone call, but, for the moment it becomes a priority (otherwise you should offer to call back later!). A great deal of time is often spent by busy people in trying to achieve impossibilities. If you can only do one thing at a time (and you can) then you must decide which task takes priority. Of course you may be progressing a number of things at the same time and this must be built into the decision.

Some things need more time spent on them than others. It may be a priority to make a promised telephone call to someone on a particular day. It will take only a few minutes. Another task, like writing this book, may well have a deadline but the work needs to be spread over a large number of days. When things change, and you accept and add a new priority, you need to recalculate. For example, if I promise to deliver the manuscript for this book on a set date and things I could not predict at the time interfere, then there are not so many options. I can work harder, long into the evening perhaps; I can delay some other task or I can delay the deadline. The temptation is to struggle on trying to do far too much for a while and then end up with something, or several somethings, done inadequately.

Those with whom you work would no doubt love it if nothing unpredictable happened in your life and you were able to do everything exactly as you wanted. For the most part they do understand that this is simply not real life; changes do occur. Realistically, to return to my example it may be better for me to say to the publisher a month ahead of the deadline, 'I am afraid I will be a week late', than to struggle on attempting to meet the time and end up not only missing it, but giving them no notice and perhaps making a mess of some other task along the way.

There is much talk these days of management stress and of managing it, books are written about it and courses conducted about it. But stress is, it seems to me, a reaction to circumstances rather than what the circumstances themselves do to you. Clear job definition and clear objectives, mentioned earlier, should make it easier to decide priorities. Certainly a realistic attitude to how you arrange your work and what gets done first, second and third makes for greater effectiveness. Nothing is achieved just by panicking or sitting around and wondering what to do or wishing the priority decision did not have to be made. Concern and constructive thought about how to sort something out are positive, just worrying about it is negative. What do all these have to do with your career?

Rapid and clear decisions made about your priorities – a continual process for most busy executives (often noted in time management systems) – will make you more effective. Clarity of thought and decisiveness are both qualities looked for in more senior management. Learning to be philosophic about the things that cause stress, and concentrate your thinking on the practicalities of what will work best, will reduce worry and allow you to get more done (remember what Samuel Johnson said: 'None but a fool worries about things he cannot influence'). The whole thrust of these last pages has been to show how increased effectiveness and the impression that it gives improves your career prospects.

Hitting targets

In many organizations the culture is, in one respect, very straightforward. People who hit targets are regarded as achieving something and doing what is required. This is most obvious where there are numbers involved. If productivity was targeted to go up 10 per cent but goes up 11 per cent instead, then this is good. And it is always clearest of all when the target is financial. It is, after all, money which keeps the wheels of commerce and industry turning, and any kind of organization solvent. So, for example, someone on the sales side consistently hitting their sales target is much more likely to be promoted than a colleague whose results are down, and consistently missing targets in such an area is often the best route to early 'retirement'. This is a powerful career influencer, and if you doubt just how powerful then, again, on the sales side you can note that it is quite often seen that the best salesperson in an organization is promoted, but may then make a poor sales manager (after all, the qualities and tasks the two jobs require are very different). Results rather than logic can sometimes drive the way things work.

The career implications of this are very clear. Because you are significantly more likely to register as doing a good job if you are consistently hitting your target (much more so than in a, perhaps apparently appealing, *laissez-faire* situation) you may want to consider:

- suggesting that your job should include some targets if it does not – especially, if possible, financial ones – or indeed putting some numbers to it and suggesting the actual targets;
- making sure any such targets are realistic, especially targets that someone else sets upon you. Some review, indeed some negotiation, here may be advisable;
- making sure any such agreed targets are regularly reviewed, and also reported, although crowing about them too loudly if they are hit may be self-defeating.

Some would even say that jobs where measurement of success is inherently difficult are to be avoided, though such a job may offer other advantages. Generally speaking, though a target hit or exceeded is always useful to the careerist, it is also motivational: most of us like to know all is going well rather than just to believe it is. The ultimate is where payment is linked to results in terms of commission or bonuses of some sort, either as a proportion of salary or sometimes with people working for commission only.

Do more than is expected of you

Exceeding expectations seems an obviously good thing, and certainly there are derogatory remarks that conjure up the opposite: we talk for instance of people 'scraping through', just doing sufficient to get by. We deride passengers and define comments such as someone meaning well as negative rather than positive.

'Getting by' is not very often the attitude upon which careers thrive. So, delivering more than others expect is, not surprisingly, to be recommended.

This does not mean, however, that work has to take over your life and that more is produced as a result of excessive hours worked. It seems to be a fact that all the jobs which are themselves interesting or worthwhile do demand more than the regular 9 to 5 attitude (certainly this is my experience, if you have found something that is interesting, pays well and makes very few demands please let me know!). So, accepting that, you need to be sufficiently industrious to create the right results and the right image. Remember there are two sides to every coin. Being consistently in the office for over-long hours could be taken as a sign of inefficiency and that you are unable to cope.

Probably the most important way to deliver more is to think more about things than is necessary just to do the job. For example, imagine you are asked to write a report on how your department's efficiency might be improved. This could be entirely introspective and based in the present, and you can come up with some perfectly good ideas for reducing costs or whatever the brief might be. Or it could take a broader view, maybe improvements are only possible by two departments working more closely together, or maybe there are advantages to be taken that link in and are made possible by events you know are coming in future. I am not suggesting the specifics of this example apply everywhere, but the process of thinking involved is clear and may well produce more.

The same principle applies to seemingly much smaller issues. I sit on a small committee, and the chairperson of it always produces and circulates in advance a detailed agenda. It is not strictly necessary in terms of the complexity of the issues, but it is useful to those present – the chairperson does just a little more than is strictly necessary; and it shows. Be known as one who operates this way and it will be one more thing that can help you to be seen in the right light.

A similar attitude might be adopted with regard to suggestions. Again from some positions this could be overdone, but sitting on your thumbs and not suggesting ideas that occur to you is no way to extend your job either. And extending it may be the first step to an improved one. Sometimes changes suggested may be simply that you will do something (perhaps for someone else) or do it in a different or better way. Sometimes they may be classic suggestions for improvement to operations or practice in some way. Remember, no system is likely to be best for ever and that there is always room for improvement and innovation, much of it driven by recognizing or predicting change, and often change outside the organization.

It is a short step from being seen as someone who does a little more than is expected, to being seen as someone with something original to contribute, to being sought out or put in a position where this can be exploited. Finally here, bear in mind how infuriating it is to see someone else implementing a change you could have suggested first but 'did not like to mention'.

Be open-minded

Nothing will stultify effectiveness and progress inside an organization more than a closed mind. There is a classic saying that you can either have, say, five years' experience, or the same year's experience repeated five times. A closed mind goes through the same processes and thus the same experience. It is a cliché to say that we live in dynamic times and that the pace of change is increasing, but that does not mean it is not true. The open-minded will cope better with changes. You will have to accept, get to grips with and use new approaches, ideas and technologies in the future. You may already see some of these looming and others may be difficult if not impossible to imagine or predict today, but they will come nevertheless.

For many, the best example of the moment is information technology (IT) with computers as a major element of it. The current generation are growing up with it and, to some extent take it in their stride. Others ignore it completely, and others still struggle to make sense of it all and progressively do so.

As a simple example, not so many years ago if someone had told me I would be typing this text, myself, on a portable computer then I would have laughed at the idea. But that is what I am now doing. I would not call myself totally computer literate by any means, but I can make it do most of the things I want, so if things suddenly go into CAPITALS or *italics* or **bold** then it is either for emphasis or to celebrate my new-found technological competence. Such a change takes time, and that is always difficult to find, more so if what you have to do is more complex. It may also sometimes be difficult (and if I knew who had written the incomprehensible manual for my laptop his or her career would come to an abrupt halt!); but it is usually worthwhile.

You must constantly take on board new ideas if your career is to progress, sometimes these will be major areas, at other times it is a question of minor, but significant points – finding a way to work with a new, and seemingly difficult colleague perhaps. Whatever the job you do there will be these changes to cope with. You must not get set in your ways so that you do not respond positively to these developments, and like so much else you must be seen to be open-minded. It will secure your effectiveness over both the short and long term and make a contribution to the way your career progresses.

8

Surviving Office Politics

'Winning isn't everything – it is the only thing.'
Vince Lombardi

THE OFFICE WHERE OFFICE POLITICS does not exist, does not exist. There are political office environments, very political ones – and not much else. It is a much more difficult area than some in which to consciously plan to excel. It contains aspects which are potentially able to exert dramatic influences – such as a company unexpectedly bought out by new owners who see change, including replacing people, as the way ahead – and over which you may have little control. If politics can have negative effects, it should not be seen either as a magic formula for success for those engaging in ruthless politicking – those able to automatically contrive their way to the top through an unstoppable series of coups (though this does happen).

On the other hand, there are some principles here that can be treated in just the same way as the other plans you make and tasks you set yourself with an eye on advancement. As you cannot ignore the politics within an organization, you must assess how you deal with it just as you would consider any other variable.

Match yourself to the corporate culture

This is meant in a practical and considered sense, and in two rather different ways that are perhaps best described by an example. First, before I set up my own business, I worked in a medium-sized consultancy firm employing about one hundred people. What made the firm profitable was having sufficient work of the right kind, at the right time and the right fee level. The culture of the firm reflected this fact. Two key ways in which people were judged were in terms of self-sufficiency – producing a volume of work they could do profitably, thus hitting or surpassing their financial targets, and sales success – producing more work than expected and thus helping compensate for others less skilful at selling. Of course, there were other things, not least quality of work. But, though it would sometimes be denied, these two were the most important, and someone doing excellent work but not hitting their target, maybe by a small margin, would not be so well regarded. Without a doubt, being self-sufficient and selling more than expected helped someone get on in the firm. Every firm has such factors as these and you would do well to think on what they are and what action you should take to get the most from the situation.

Secondly, though perhaps less practically linked to the work of organizations, there are other, more social factors. An organization may build up a cadre of senior people who all share the same interests or activities. In one firm, this may mean many internal decisions are made on the golf course, or in a particular bar after office hours. In another it might mean overseas activity is favoured, in part, because of senior people's love of travel. This may be more difficult to fit in with, and you may not be instantly welcomed into the 'inner sanctum' simply by taking up golf, for example; but it should be observed and considered.

This is less a question of being what is called a 'company man', than of taking the most practical opportunities offered (the consultancy example above is a good one in this respect); apart from anything else you do not want to be seen to be striving to fit in in a contrived way, as this can be self-defeating in terms of the effect it will have on others.

Sex

When Stephen Hawkings was writing his now famous book about cosmology – *A Brief History of Time* – he was told that every mathematical formula he included would halve its sales. He risked one, and it went on to sell millions. Conversely, I am told, that if the word 'sex' is in the contents of a book it is good for sales. But there are other reasons to include this here. Both men and women have careers, but it is simply not true to suggest that circumstances are the same for both.

This has been touched on earlier, when it was suggested that women must work harder at being accepted and at getting on. Not all organizations are less than women-friendly, of course, but some are (and some may put men at a disadvantage). Here is not the place to debate the morality of this. Of course we all essentially believe in being fair, but we also notice that in so many ways the world is just not fair. Given that, what are the career implications?

We come back to assessment. Everyone, male and female, needs to assess the corporate culture in which they work and see what action it suggests. There are companies in which women are simply much less likely to succeed. A woman has various options ranging from fighting it, trying harder or looking for a more compatible environment in which to forge a career.

Having said that, all the other comments in this book may help anyone, regardless of gender. It is also possible for a woman to blame her sex for a lack of promotion, when in fact the blame should be laid on lack of competence or bad decisions in the past. The job environment is tough. It is tough for everyone, regardless of sex. And it is tough because most organizations operate in competitive marketplaces, with competition waiting to take advantage of any weakness.

So, there are many circumstances where human preferences, or failings, influence things so that a woman may be promoted because she is good looking or screened out because someone sees her (albeit wrongly) as having less commitment than a man, and there may be ways round this. The modern career woman is more than a match for much of the possible prejudice she will meet. But, whatever the circumstance, a person will do better in their career if they plan to, and many of the approaches and actions advocated here are more likely to create an edge which gets you ahead than any accident of gender.

Prejudice takes many forms. Yes, there are those who will rate people less highly because they are the wrong sex, or race, because they are homosexual, or too young or too old, or not from the right background, or . . . . the list could go on. I even heard of one manager who had a mark on the door of his office and would not even interview anyone for a job unless they topped the mark in height! Personally I am not sure I would want to work for anyone who was so irrational as to, say, only employ people who were of a particular astrological star sign. There is a difference between action – some of it in the form of a long-term campaign – to create an atmosphere in which such prejudices no longer thrive, and the action an individual takes when faced with a particular form of it.

This is not the place to set out the details, but these are areas that are now covered by law, either employment legislation or more general regulation. Many organizations now have enlightened ways of dealing with issues such as sexual harassment or bullying, and if they have not then the law may provide an answer.

There are various options, but one that should always make a difference is activity that purposefully seeks to develop a career based on practical aspects, actions that make you the best person for the job simply because you can do it better than anyone else.

Assess and know the opposition

Teamwork is an essential skill of any successful enterprise. Yet it is simply not true to imagine that an organization is one big, happy family with everyone sharing the same feelings and ambitions. All organizations are to some degree or another hierarchical, and most are pyramid shaped. There are, as has been said, more Indians than Chiefs. Inevitably therefore, people within an organization are in competition with each other, and how you progress will be influenced by how others – particularly those with similar intentions – progress.

Your own career plans should therefore reflect an active and ongoing appraisal of the fact that competition is inherent. Who is especially likely to influence your progress in the particular direction you have set your sights on? And how are they likely to proceed with their career plan? Honest and open competition (though there are always unseen undercurrents) is to be expected. However, out-and-out politicking is much less to be recommended, though of course it happens, and if the knives are out then self-defence has to be the order of the day. Unfortunately this kind of approach tends to be bad for the organization, breeding suspicion, low motivation and resulting in more time being spent watching backs than on the job in hand. It can also create confusion which is similarly distracting from the real tasks and issues (which reminds me of a delegate on a course saying: 'In my company we are so confused we are stabbing each other in the chest!' – some will know the feeling).

However things proceed, you should take competitive elements, in particular the people involved, into your thinking and act in a way that assesses realistically how it all changes the situation. Sometimes such an assessment will send you off on another track, or into another organization, for there are those where the cut and thrust is simply too much. On other occasions you have to resolve and gear up for fierce competition. Remember, success would be no fun if it were too easy!

Watch for signs of likely change

Horror stories abound of signs of impending doom. In one American company, the signs of your personal position faltering were said to be organized with the telephone. Occasionally someone would sit down at their desk and find the phone was dead. On contacting the operator to report the fact (using another phone), a polite voice would inform them that they no longer needed a telephone. Unpleasant. Here I mean to commend the simple, practical advice of keeping an ear to the ground and your wits about you.

Certain people have been heard to say they are too busy for politics, usually just before something occurs to their disadvantage which they would have seen coming a mile away if they had only looked up. Being busy, for whatever reason – and I have commended elsewhere being productive as a means to success – must not blind you to what is going on around you. I once saw some office graffiti which said, 'It is difficult to see the writing on the wall if your back's to it.' It is a fair point.

Of course, you must also take a constructive view. The reason to watch for signs is only in part to watch for warning signs; it is also to watch for opportunities. For example, in one company two executives worked closely together and got on well. One day the more senior of the two confided that he was seeking to work overseas. 'In a year or so I will be on the other side of the world', he said. On the day he duly resigned to move abroad, his colleague was able to put a detailed and considered report on their joint boss's desk recommending he took over as the department head, showing why he was well equipped to do so, taking the department on, and how he could rapidly re-staff to fill the gap his colleague would leave. What is more, during that year when he knew what was likely to occur, he took some self-development action to make sure he had a good chance of the plan being approved. Is that office politics or sensibly taking advantage of circumstances?

Display symbols (or not)

Somebody once coined the term 'executive toys' for desk gadgetry of various sorts; primarily for the tacky type such as those things that roll stainless steel balls into holes marked 'Yes' and 'No' to aid decision-making. The choice of such things, if any, should be treated with care. Some people go to some pains to cultivate an image in this way, ensuring that they have the right newspapers or magazines around the office, that their computer is visible, that the clock shows three different time zones, and the wall and bookshelves are stocked with the right kind of pictures, certificates, and business titles to show that the office is occupied by a thrusting and high-powered executive.

The trouble is that many things of this kind can backfire. The clock may not be seen as a symbol of international connections but as pretentious. Someone who has actually read one of the books (which you have not) might ask you about its content and so on. Probably the only reasonable advice is moderation and care. Personally I would settle for surroundings that are straightforward and businesslike, rather than risk something being taken the wrong way.

Linking back to time management and organization, a tidy desk speaks of efficiency. Too tidy and it looks as if you do nothing, but a real mess does not heighten your image. Find the right blend of organization and activity, and be sure you can find things easily when certain others may be there to witness your search.

None of this means your work area, whether office or open-plan workstation, cannot have a few homely touches, though it is good if even they have some genuine relevance to what you do. Amongst other things on my office wall is a print showing an original illustration from Lewis Carroll's famous book *Alice in Wonderland*. The words reproduced below the picture of Alice in conversation with the Cheshire Cat run as follows:

> 'Would you tell me, please, which way I ought to go from here?'
>
> 'That depends a good deal on where you want to get to', said the Cat.
>
> 'I don't very much care where . . .', said Alice.
>
> 'Then it doesn't matter which way you go', said the Cat.
>
> ' – so long as I get somewhere', Alice added as an explanation.
>
> 'Oh, you're sure to do that', said the Cat, 'if only you walk long enough.'

As a plea for clear objectives this is not a bad motto for a business; or for a career. Anyway, *I* like it.

Trust and honesty

Earlier we looked at assessing the opposition, but took a reasonable view of opposition as those who are for whatever reason in competition with you, directly or indirectly. Sometimes however, and it pays to be realistic about this, opposition has an altogether more sinister meaning to it. What is the saying? 'Just because you are paranoid doesn't mean people aren't out to get you' – many a true word is spoken in jest and organizations can sometimes have something about them of the law of the jungle. Some people, though only a few, one hopes, are destructive for no good reason, or are spiteful or, for whatever reason, are just not on your side and happy to see you fall by the wayside.

I do not wish to give the impression that this is a major factor (much less encourage unpleasant in-fighting) but this book would be incomplete if it omitted any reference to the possibility. Advice? You should be, in a word, watchful. Read between the lines, take a little while to form views of people, be especially wary in difficult or changing times – adversity sometimes brings out the worst in people – and treat remarks like 'Trust me' with a healthy degree of caution. There may not be an assassin hiding around every corner, but you may well meet one or two over the longer term. Forewarned is forearmed.

'Honesty is the best policy' and in business this is usually the case. I suppose I must say 'usually', because it is sadly true to say there are some people in some organizations who rise up the ranks and do well from out and out deception. It happens – and many of us have probably come across people who fall into this category. Not only that, but there are areas where large numbers of people are regularly dishonest. For instance, research in the UK has shown that more than fifteen per cent of people applying for new jobs complete the necessary application forms dishonestly. This does not just include minor embellishments, some people claim to have degrees from universities which they have never attended, to have worked for organizations they have never even visited, and twice I have heard of people being taken on to do jobs where they received and needed to use a company car – and only then was it discovered that their claim to be able to drive was a lie!

So the truth of the matter is that, while you may prosper by lying, you only have to get found out once and any good it may have done in the past is lost for ever. In any case most people want to achieve whatever they do on their own merits; there can surely be no real and lasting satisfaction in conning your way through. I once met a manager on a training programme whose company appraisal system, which rated many performance criteria on a ten-point scale, had honesty amongst the factors listed. I did not see the sense of this, and said so: in most organizations you cannot rate people from 1 to 10 for honesty, even if you wanted to. You are either honest or you are fired.

So, honesty is surely the best policy. Not least, people around you should know that you are honest and that you keep your word, honesty links to trust which is an important factor in getting on in any organization.

Being political in the sense of being aware of all that goes on is clearly useful, at least some of your tactics will be affected by the prevailing political climate. Becoming the office Machiavelli probably holds out more likelihood of disaster than rewards.

9

What You See

'Only fools do not judge by appearances.'
Oscar Wilde

IT IS SOMETIMES SAID, for example of advertising, that 'perception is reality'. In other words, people will usually base their judgement on what they see of something. So too with people. Think of someone in your organization, perhaps whom you do not know very much about. Ask yourself what you think about them: are they busy? Competent? Approachable? Expert? Ambitious? Efficient? What do you think their staff think of them? And more. You will find that if you make yourself draw conclusions from whatever evidence is visible, a reasonable picture seems to build up. You feel that you can judge something about them.

Whether it is true or not is, of course, another matter.

Your very visibility gives out many signals, and will do so whether you consciously think about it or not. Here we review some of the ways in which you can give signals that paint the right kind of picture of you in a career-enhancing way, one that will create an image compatible with your future career intentions.

Looking the part

I once attended an evening talk of a professional institute and heard someone give a review of what are sometimes called 'beauty parades', that is pitches or competitive presentations. The speaker made a number of interesting points including the simple advice: look the part. He then gave a number of detailed examples, one of which was the advice for men to wear what he called 'big-boy shoes' (ones with shoelaces rather than slip-on style). Now this is going a bit far perhaps, but the point is well made – first impressions are largely visual and they are important. So too is someone's prevailing style, manner (confidence etc.), everything that contributes to how colleagues and others see you around the office and work environment. That this is certainly thought about is verified by language – you may regularly hear people using expressions such as the 'interview suit' when they speak of an important occasion.

Now this is a difficult area to advise on precisely. I am not promoting designer fashion or any specific style of dress, and you have to be reasonably natural, but you want to be seen to take business seriously.

You can be smart without spending a fortune, you must always be clean and tidy, and the details matter. The Americans, who have a jargon phrase for everything, talk about 'power dressing'. This is a concept that is too contrived for many, indeed there is a real likelihood that going too far in this way becomes self-defeating, and is just seen as pretentious. It may be important in some jobs to meet the standards and style of those with whom the organization does business, rather than internally; for example customers. Once having met with a major bank to discuss possible training work, a colleague of mine, one who took a pride in his appearance, was dismayed when a letter came back requesting that the work be done by someone 'shorter in the hair and longer in the tooth'! An older and more traditional alternative was found and the work went well; that is the client's right. Horses for courses.

So, what specifically is certain? The following are often mentioned:

- Clean finger nails and neat hair.
- Smart (rather than over-fashionable) clothes.
- Clean shoes.
- A smart, and tidy, briefcase.

Also, though it is more difficult to judge, an appropriate spend on both wardrobe and any other visible elements (I once had an enquiry from someone who said: 'One of your competitors has just been to see me and arrived in a Porsche: I think I would like another quote').

Finally, styles and norms differ internationally – a suit is normal business dress in the UK, a jacket and trousers (not a matching suit) is seen as just as acceptable as a suit in Holland, shirts and ties are more important in countries like say Singapore, where the hot weather precludes jackets – and the norms differ in different kinds of business – a bank, for example, being more formal than an advertising agency. Similarly men and women have different styles to consider, with the greater range of choices facing women frankly making their decisions more difficult.

Whatever your style, whatever you opt for, think about it and remember your appearance says very much more about you than you might think. You do not want to get hung up over every item you wear or use – from shoes to laptop and its carrying case, but you will have an image; the only question is, what image will you make it?

Create external visibility

On one of the comparatively few times I have done a radio interview, I remember meeting another interviewee who was there to comment on some technical matter. We got chatting and I asked him who he was. He said that he worked for a large company and had made a point of becoming known as the company's expert on the particular technical issue in question. 'Do you run the technical department?' I asked him. 'No,' he said, 'but I shall one day.' Investigating what he did to establish himself as the technical guru, I was inclined to believe him.

This anecdote makes a good point – public relations is not only a valuable tool to promote the company, there is a corresponding process which has career development potential as well. It is tightly linked with some of the communications skills reviewed earlier. My fellow interviewee at the radio studio would not have been there unless he could talk fluently about his chosen topic, but just being knowledgeable about it was not enough, he had to actively create the opportunity; and perhaps do so more powerfully than other, more obvious, choices for spokesperson. What is more, if he performed well then he stood a good chance of being asked back. It is an area where one thing can satisfyingly lead to another once you have created some momentum.

Radio is perhaps a dramatic example to take, though by no means an unattainable one, but public relations activity generally incorporates many different possibilities. Given that you have, or can create, some expertise worthy of comment, and very many jobs have this possibility, start internally as you review the possibilities. Is there a company magazine or newsletter? Are there groups or committees you can take part in or speak at?

Then externally: should you be seeking to write articles, lecture at the local management institute or speak at a trade or professional body meeting? This is very much an activity that creates its own momentum. For example, an article published in the company newsletter might be adapted to go in an external publication, a copy of that sent to a professional body might prompt an invitation to speak, and at that meeting you might meet someone who . . . but you get the point.

If such activity grows up naturally, and has a use for the organization as well as for you, then it should not create ripples (though others may well wish they had thought of it first) and it can become an ongoing part of what you do to indicate to those about you that you are going places. If your organization has a public relations department, or if it uses a PR agency, then it may be worth creating contact and establishing a relationship with them (most are happy to investigate any help offered, make what you offer useful and they will keep in touch). Work *with* others like this and the potential number of opportunities and methods multiplies.

Nothing succeeds like success, and being seen to have achieved these things is certainly potentially useful. See you in the studio.

Take an interest in your interests

In some companies, particularly large ones, there is considerable social interaction among staff. Just how much there is and how it works will vary, and is affected by such things as whether there is a social club and where the office is located: some city centre locations where people typically travel long distances to work may mean they live as much as a hundred miles apart and this will reduce the social possibilities. There will also be a culture within the organization relating to this kind of activity. In some companies, senior people are involved in some of this and others are clearly expected to be too. In others, it is seen as a lower-level activity and you may not want to get too involved in case you are seen as essentially frivolous.

Another issue here is that, rightly or wrongly, executives have a total image. Though interference in employees' private lives is not the style of many organizations, and would be (indeed is) resented by many staff, you may be expected to have certain interests. Some of these are perfectly reasonable; it is useful for executives, especially those who have contact outside the firm, to be generally well informed in terms of current affairs, for example. If you are in a technical area, you may need to keep up-to-date on a broad range of scientific matters simply to be able to relate well to others you work with.

On the other hand, there are organizations where the style of the chief executive – evidenced by a passion for, say, golf, science fiction or undersea diving – is mirrored by aspiring staff around the office forever plunging into the sea or reading Arthur C. Clarke. Whether this last is useful or not is uncertain. I would like to think it is not, but there are organizations where this kind of fitting-in is important. It is certainly worth a thought. You are unlikely to have to rearrange your whole life around such things, but some accommodation with such perceptions may be useful.

Sex: avoiding problems

Sex – again (this should guarantee even more sales). But no, this section will not provide a guide to your love life. It is here for a reason, because the gender of any individual inevitably has an effect on how they are seen. This is no place for a major debate on women in business, suffice it to repeat that they are, in many cultures, apt not to be taken as seriously as men. Leaving the reasons on one side, what is the effect? Let me start with an illustration. I used to have a young lady working with me who moved from a secretarial position to one of more executive responsibility and then to a position where she joined a small management committee. Halfway through the first meeting she attended, someone delivered a tray of tea and coffee and left it on a side table. Discussion continued and, after a few minutes, she got up, poured and handed round the drinks.

After the meeting, she asked me how she had got on. She had done well, contributing some sound comments, but I remember saying, 'Why did you pour the tea?' She did not hesitate, saying at once, 'Right, I won't do that again.' Now I am not suggesting that every woman early in a management career is in danger of being typecast as the tea lady, or secretary/hostess, and it did not in fact matter who did the pouring-out chore; the point is that perceptions stick. Sometimes women are in danger of being underrated and thus, rightly or wrongly, women have to think twice as hard as men about how they are seen. So in my view, she was right to attend to this sort of detail, rather than dismiss it as not mattering or overreacting (for the record, her subsequent progress proved she was ultimately very much seen in the right light).

Similarly, and for members of either sex, there is merit in making sure all dealings around the organization are on the basis of jobs done, expertise and merit rather than gender. However, I do not suppose anything I might write will prevent the occasional normal social interaction, and in organizations the world over, people will continue to say: 'How about dinner?' Though there are no doubt cases of liaisons (which some organizations frown on, or actively seek to prevent) having ulterior motives, as a general rule regarding them as anything to do with career development runs the risk of getting you into very deep water.

Do not drink to excess

This is common sense, but worth a word. In many businesses, a certain amount of socializing is not only pleasant, it is part of the way the business works. On the other hand few, if any, decisions, communications or interactions are helped by being the worse for drink; and most, if not all, managements will prefer to promote the office cat before promoting someone with even a single suspicion of a drinking problem. Enough said.

Give rather than take

It would be difficult and, given the many different types of job and styles of organization in the world, not even helpful to set out a perfect mix of characteristics for those wanting to develop their careers. One point is, however, worth a thought. It may seem that a dedication to developing a career demands a selfish outlook, and to some degree this may be true. But think also of the effect a selfish attitude in others has on you. It is not the most endearing characteristic imaginable.

Success and effectiveness are assisted by co-operation: teamwork has been mentioned elsewhere, and a selfish attitude to others hardly makes their co-operation in ways that will help you or your organizational objectives a foregone conclusion.

When I first went into the consultancy field, I worked with a group of people who were less selfish than any other I have encountered before or since. No one ever seemed too busy to help. You could walk into any office and get advice, information and support of all kinds – from just a word to a complete run-down on something (if it was impossible to help immediately then a time was set when a discussion could be made to suit). Information was regarded as for sharing, not for exclusive hoarding, and the whole firm, far from grinding to a halt because time was taken up in this way, seemed to thrive on the attitude. For a newcomer, it was a godsend and I made full use of the learning and accelerated experience it provided and, in due course, found myself part of the network spending time giving as well as receiving.

There is an altruistic side to this attitude. You never know in an organization how things will go and how things will turn out. The person whose head you bite off today because they want a moment of your time when you are busy, turns up next a year later in a position of authority or influence and with not the slightest intention of sharing anything with you. You cannot have too many allies. A point was made earlier about assessing and dealing with the opposition. The reverse – assessing and building bridges with potential allies – applies also and some time may be well spent on this. It helps your job now and it could well help your future.

Avoid being typecast

Every kind of business activity seems to run this risk. In my own business, it is very difficult to stop some clients seeing me exclusively as a consultant, others seeing me exclusively as a trainer, or a writer (though I work at creating a more rounded image!). Some companies have a similar problem in selling the range of what they make; they are known for one, or two, main products and the other lines always seem to get left behind. There can be a similar situation with people as a career progresses, and sometimes the effect can be negative.

For example, the Greeks (or was it the Romans?) used to execute any messengers bringing bad news. It cannot have made the bad news go away but it must, I suppose, have made them all feel a bit better; well, all except the messengers! In a company people can take on a series of tasks. Tasks which play to their strengths are important and have to be done, but can tend to create a negative image of the individual. If you become known as the person who closed down the troublesome plant, made 300 people redundant, axed the firm's oldest and dearest product, and cancelled the research everyone felt would herald a new era of successful innovation – then you are perhaps not going to be the most popular person in the company.

Now there is considerable danger in making decisions in order to be popular, and I am not suggesting either that hard decisions

should not be faced or should be fudged. Equally there are professional troubleshooters who do nothing but this sort of thing and
manage to retain a positive profile in the organization for which
they work (perhaps because they operate with some sensitivity). But
one still might conclude that there are certain activities and tasks
that are better avoided if your subsequent profile and career are not
to be blighted. Even if the blight is small you may be better without
it. It would be invidious to offer more specific advice but the point is
worth keeping in mind, and should you feel exposed in this kind of
way at least you can take action to re-balance the effect.

Overall, it pays to bear in mind the many factors and activities
that contribute to the way you are seen. With some it is simply a
question of exaggerating some trait to fit in with someone else; for
example, if your boss is the sort of person who has a considerable
need to focus on the details, it may be useful to extend your natural
inclination so that you appear equally concerned.

There may be areas mentioned here that you feel you can usefully consider further; indeed you may well be able to think of
additional areas also where attention could also benefit the way you
are perceived.

10 Management Strengths

'Nothing is so embarrassing as watching someone do something that you said couldn't be done.'

Sam Ewing

MANY PEOPLE WHO WORK in an organization find that progress involves an increasing responsibility for managing other people. This is natural enough given the structure of most organizations. In some jobs, based on a specialist expertise, progress seems to involve a situation where the work involved consists less and less of the specialist expertise and more and more of management and administration. It is, however, easier to develop administrative skills than to develop management ones. In any case management is – or will be – for most a prime career skill and worth some comments here. The points in this chapter are not intended to be any kind of comprehensive review of how to be a manager – there are other ways of looking into that – but are designed to highlight those factors that have a direct bearing on your ability to do the job and progress your career.

Management is a complex set of skills and processes, and effective management is another of those things in business life which does not just happen. Good managers may make it look easy; but this is deceptive. They need to work at it and only by having a clear view of what is necessary, and being prepared to give the whole process the time and consideration it demands, can they make it appear to happen without a problem. So the first rule is to take any necessity to become involved in management very seriously indeed.

Some people see management as an end in itself, they obtain challenge and satisfaction from managing a team of people and producing results from their efforts (a good definition of management is that it is achieving results *through other people*; it is thus very different from what you actually do *yourself*). Others find the whole process a distraction from whatever they see as the real job in hand. If you are in the latter category, then make no mistake, it is not something you can ignore; if management is a necessary part of the job you do or even a job you do en route to something else, then you have to do it and do it well. Nothing will show you up in a worse light than being in charge of a group of people who become unhappy and demotivated because they are poorly managed; more so if they perform poorly as a result.

Overall, the management process must successfully influence your people to ensure they implement an agreed plan, and do so effectively. It has to blend setting up the tasks involved, and doing so in a way that works with the individuals and also respects the entity of the team involved. Your skills in achieving the required results through the group must be matched by your skill in managing the relationships of individuals within the team.

The essentials of the management process are:

- *Defining objectives*: identifying tasks, restraints and setting targets.
- *Planning*: and deciding priorities.
- *Communicating*: to brief, instruct and check understanding.
- *Supporting and control*: monitoring progress, checking and adapting.
- *Evaluating*: reviewing whether and how results have been achieved.
- *Linking to the future*: experience should affect the future.

All this should be done in a way that focuses separately on the task, and the needs of the individuals involved as well as the team.

You should make excellence in management your goal, it will reflect well on every aspect of your career. The further points in this chapter look at individual aspects of the process that are important in this way.

Work *with* your people, not *against* them

Of course managers must manage. It does not just happen, and results are important. But some managers seem to have or develop a very confrontational style (I know, I once worked for one) which is, in my view, much less likely to produce results and is certainly less motivational for all involved.

You will achieve most by ensuring that your team performs effectively. If you treat people as competition, if you restrict rather than encourage what they do, there is a good chance they will perform less well; and remember that as a manager their results reflect on you – whatever they are. You must work with a team, through a team and you need their support. Think of managers whom you have worked for in the past, or at present. What are the characteristics you like? Do you want to work for someone from whom you learn something (often the top-rated desired characteristic in a boss), who delegates rather than keeps everything to themselves, who gives the credit rather than takes it, who is fair, not secretive? You can probably think of many more criteria. Whatever you put on such a list, consider also what others might list. What do they want from you as a manager? None of this means you cannot be firm where necessary, run a tight ship and not suffer fools gladly; management may well need such attitudes as well, but the whole effect must come over in a way that carries people with you.

You must not let people try to run before they can walk, but with things properly set up if you give them their head they may well give you a great deal more.

Help people develop

This is important; no one wants to do the same job repetitively for ever and ever any more than you do. Market and environment factors in any case make most jobs dynamic, keeping up with the changes is part of what must happen, so jobs should not become static. But people respond to a challenge, they want to learn, to do new things and old things better, and this must not be seen as a threat. There is a real fear in some managers that allowing people to develop risks their taking the credit, if not taking over. Two points need considering here: first, managing a team means just that, the manager cannot do everything, indeed the effectiveness of the section is dependent on the productivity of the whole team. If you do not delegate, or develop others to do more and more, little progress will be possible. If you do, then some of the work moves out of your hands but the effectiveness of the whole effort will increase, and the potential of a team that performs well far outstrips that of any one individual.

Secondly, there is a valuable maxim to the effect that management cannot have the authority and the credit. This means that trying to organize so that everything reflects well on you achieves less than giving the credit to others. As what they do expands, you take your own credit in terms of respect for a well-managed team producing results. Developing others, with all that that entails, will develop your results and your recognition.

Actively motivate people

Motivation is a complex set of principles and processes within the overall management task. Put simply, people perform best when they enjoy what they do and feel it is worthwhile and appreciated. This is again, like so much else, not something that happens of its own volition. Motivation takes time, and it is time that some managers begrudge, feeling that time is better spent 'actually doing something' rather than 'helping people along who should be able to look after themselves'.

But we cannot change human nature. People need motivation, and the time spent on what is a continuous process is well worthwhile in terms of the difference it makes to results. This is a well-researched area, you must not believe that it is different in your group and thus motivation is something that can be avoided. What must be done, and how, is too big a topic to go into comprehensively in the space available here. Suffice to say that motivation must minimize those aspects of work that tend to worry people (called dissatisfiers, and concerned primarily with environmental factors such as policy, administration and work conditions), and maximize the impact of those things that create good feelings (the motivators, which are mainly job related with the most important usually being regarded as achievement and recognition).

Some of these demand action with people on an individual basis, some with the team, ranging from the simplest form of motivation: just saying 'Thank you' or 'Well done' (and how many of us who are managers can really put our hand on our heart and say we do this sufficiently often – yet everyone hates being taken for granted), to complex reward schemes, incentives and other more tangible tactics.

Managing in an environment of low motivation is twice as hard as when things are going well in this respect. Attitude and thus, in turn, performance are directly affected by the motivational climate. Do not neglect this area: a good team is an asset to the career of anyone with management responsibilities.

Keep in touch

Successful management cannot be conducted from behind a closed office door. If you are to have a well-motivated team, if you are to achieve results, create and maintain satisfactory quality standards – whatever you have to do, you have to be in touch with the people. It was the American book *In Search of Excellence* which coined the phrase 'management by walking about' (MBWA) which means exactly what it says, coupled with the recommendation that you do not just see people, you *talk* to them – and *listen* too.

This happens in two ways. First, you have to be accessible. People need to be able to come to you when necessary (not to waste time when they should be able to cope), they should feel free, indeed be encouraged, to make suggestions, feed in ideas and contribute in whatever ways make sense to the smooth running of the operation in which all are involved.

Second, you have to go to them, and this takes more effort if they are not nearby, for the principle is the same whether the people concerned are in the next-door office, in the field like salesmen or engineers, or in another office or location – which may be an office a short drive away or your operation's overseas outpost. You have to see what they are up to, be seen to do so, check how things are going, understand the situation on their ground and be sufficiently informed as a result to make the decisions you need to do, and do so wisely.

Again this will not only contribute to the results you make happen, it is the right way to be seen and has added career benefits in the sense that you really know what is going on across a broad front.

There is a saying that you do not have to be able to lay eggs to be a chicken farmer! Similarly you do not have to be able to do all the tasks those in your team have to undertake, but it surely helps if you understand something about them all, and the people doing them, and if this knowledge is up to date. So resolve to be the sort of manager who walks about, and does so regularly and with purpose.

Adopt the right management style

No two managers manage in exactly the same way, nor is there some textbook form of doing so which should be followed slavishly, much less one that would be right for every circumstance. Quite apart from anything else, you cannot make yourself work in a way that is simply contrary to your normal instincts and manner. Style could be taken as encompassing everything that is done in managing, but here I want to concentrate on only three points, not least because I feel they are of dual importance to both effective management and a style of management that is likely to be approved by others and thus benefit your career.

Be fair. There are few things that people dislike more in a manager than unfairness. This is not, however, the same as being democratic (few organizations are and it is not usually any recipe for decisive or appropriate action). But to treat people on a similar basis, not play favourites, and be seen only to make decisions for the benefit of the general good has to be right.

Be consistent. To a degree, this goes with being fair and a first comment is necessarily similar: people hate working for someone who runs hot and cold, who is all sweetness and light one minute and fire and brimstone the next. So a consistent approach gets the best from people, and this certainly relates somewhat obviously to promotion decisions – would you select someone for a job if they were very inconsistent in this way or would you see it as taking a disproportionate risk? The latter seems most likely.

Be consultative. All the best advice about management style seems to indicate that the days of a dictatorial approach, one that simply tells people what to do, have long gone. People expect to be consulted to some extent (though my earlier point about democracy stands). Not only that, but only through consultation and discussion can you orchestrate the full power of your people in terms of ideas and effectiveness. It takes more time than just issuing instructions, but in the long run if more goes well as a result (and if people are encouraged to make positive input it will) this will save time.

What you do here needs some conscious thought and considered action. In career terms too you can do worse than observe and analyse what seems to be the preferred style of management (by looking at the kinds of people who are moving successfully up the hierarchy, who may well share certain approaches; indeed there is a phenomenon called mirror recruitment through which management only select people who exhibit all their own characteristics, good or bad!). So, whilst you should not copy an organizational style slavishly, it may well be worth accommodating certain clearly preferred characteristics.

Good, effective management is likely to exhibit fairness, decisiveness, loyalty to staff and others and to the organization, and expertise. Managers must be honest, consistent in approach, and may sometimes need to be courageous; people like it too if they are good delegators, not too secretive and treat people as people, rather than cogs in the corporate machine.

The reality is often very different with indecisive managers passing off others' ideas as their own, playing politics, holding people in check (especially if they see them as a threat), manipulating things to their own advantage and passing the buck.

Performance appraisals

Managers are responsible for their people, and that includes the job of assessing and reporting on how they are performing. This is a management task and logically falls into this chapter, but in reviewing something about it we will consider the career advantages to be obtained from being appraised, as well as something about the process itself.

This is not the place for me to commend to organizations the merits of a good appraisal system, one that makes a constructive contribution to maintaining and improving performance standards, though it may be worth noting that in my experience you are likely to encounter different kinds of appraisal in a career that spans a number of different employers. Not all of them will be effective: some managers are bad at conducting such meetings, and you may feel not all are constructive. Careers do not progress in a perfect world, but you should seek to get the most from all appraisals, whatever they are like.

Preparing for appraisals

Appraisals are a waste of time if they are not constructive, and if badly conducted can be divisive and awkward as well. Any manager needing to conduct one should prepare carefully.

As someone about to be appraised, be sure you understand how the appraisal system in your organization works before you find yourself in the first such meeting. Incidentally, this is a good topic to investigate when you are being interviewed for a job, asking how appraisal is regarded and how it is done. But before your first meeting you are likely to need more detailed information than is spelt out at that stage. Ask for information if this is not provided and ask some of your longer-serving peers how their meetings go, how long they last and what they get from them. Particularly be sure you know *why* appraisals are done, how management conducting them views them, what they look to get from them, and what time-span the review covers. Then you can consider how you want your meeting to go and how you can influence it. For instance ask yourself:

- what you want to raise and discuss;
- what is likely to be raised (and responses to any negative areas that may come up);
- what the link is between appraisal and development and training, and what you hope to get organized in this area;
- what the link is between the meeting and your future work, responsibilities and projects undertaken;
- what questions you want to ask.

If it is not your first appraisal, also check what was said at, and documented after, the last one. This must be done in the context of what you now know about the forthcoming appraisal. A couple of points are worth careful planning. One is the link to salary review and other benefits. Many organizations separate discussion of this from appraisal meetings (indeed there is a strong case for doing so); if this is the case it cannot be raised, except perhaps in general terms.

If rewards will be discussed you may want to check a whole range of things: the level of inflation, the level of pay offered by competitors, changing practice (or taxation rules) with regard to benefits in kind. But remember that employers do not tend to pay for costs incurred in having a family, moving so that your travel costs go up, or any other personal matter. In most areas pay is a matter of comparisons – the 'going rate' – and performance. So the best way to create a case for a rise is by documenting what you have achieved.

Another key point is the make-up of the discussion in terms of time scale. A good appraisal will always spend more time on the future than on the past: both aspects need thought and certainly there is no excuse for your not having the facts at your fingertips about anything that is a likely topic for discussion in the review of past events.

Make notes as you plan, and take them with you to the meeting – there is no point in trusting key matters to memory and, in any case, being seen to have thought seriously about the meeting will benefit you. You may only get one, sometimes two, such opportunities in any one year. Therefore, some careful preparation will prevent these occasions being wasted.

During the meeting

The person who is conducting the appraisal will have a bearing on both how it is done and how you need to conduct yourself. If it is with a manager with whom you are on good terms and whom you see every day, this will make for a less formal meeting than if it is someone more senior with whom you only have occasional contact (many appraisals involve two or even three people plus the person to be appraised).

A good appraisal will:

- be notified well in advance;
- have a clear agenda;
- have a likely duration in mind.

These are things you should ask for if necessary. In particular you may have ideas about how much time will be spent discussing last year and the next, how interactive the meeting is and when you can ask questions. You may also wish to know what is, and is not, on the record. Some appraisals are rather like a checklist in style, that is the appraiser leads and raises the points one at a time, asking for your view or comment. Others are more open and allow the person being appraised to lead, pulling them back to an agenda only if the meeting digresses too much. Ideally you will know which way it runs, but you must be ready for either. Remember, any lack of comment may be read as lack of awareness, knowledge or as indecisiveness. On the other hand, if any question posed needs some thought then it is better to let the appraiser know rather than answering with a hasty comment.

Appraisals should not be traumatic occasions. If they are constructive – and prompting change in the future is the only real reason for doing them, and that is unlikely to happen unless they are – then you can take a reasonably relaxed view of them (provided you have done some preparation) and there is no reason why you should not enjoy them as well as find them useful. You are on show, career planning decisions are being made, albeit long term, by those conducting these meetings, but it is also a positive opportunity for you to present something of your competence in a way that goes 'on the record'.

Appraisals: the follow-up

Appraisals are too important to just file away in your mind or forget about once they are past. They can provide a catalyst to an ongoing dialogue during the year. In many organizations, the system demands that the appraiser documents proceedings, and usually that the appraisee confirms that this documentation is a true record of the salient issues.

But there is no reason why you cannot take the initiative on particular matters. Consider the following as an example. Development requirements are one topic which most appraisals review. This may result in specific action – 'I will enrol you on that presentations skills course next month' – or it may result in further discussion, more than can be accommodated in the appraisal meeting itself. It may be useful to volunteer to undertake the processes involved (remember your boss could have a dozen appraisals in the same week and much attendant administration). If you put in a paper setting out some suggestions for action, and if this is then used as the agenda for another session about it, then this could well see more of what you plan happening sooner than would otherwise be the case. Similarly, use the opportunity to report back after any agreed training, in writing or at a meeting, so that the dialogue continues. If the training has been agreed as successful then there is logic in discussing 'what's next'.

A final point – you may think attending them is a chore, but appraisals are not easy to conduct (as you may know or one day find out). They take time to prepare and always seem to be scheduled during busy periods. So, if yours has been useful, express your thanks, and if it has not, try to comment in a way that may set the scene for a more productive encounter next year.

Accept and learn from criticism

A good appraisal is likely to be a good meeting. Even if it is poorly conducted and not really very constructive, it is a satisfying feeling to come out saying to yourself, 'I did well', particularly when someone else has told you so. But unless you believe the graffiti which says 'I used to be great but now I am absolutely perfect', few of us get through many such meetings without having to take some criticism. We must consider the possibility that it is fair comment. You are probably not perfect, you do not get everything right or excel in all you do, and you sometimes get things wrong.

Because, perhaps understandably, no one likes having their failures, even minor ones, aired in public, there is a danger that you simply put such comment out of your mind and concentrate on the good things that are said (almost all appraisals will touch on both). But careers are not enhanced either by repeating mistakes or ignoring failings or weaknesses. If you do not take prompt action after an appraisal, at least in terms of planning such action, then the moment will pass, a mistake may repeat, and results – and your career – may suffer. Resolve to take note and, if necessary, take action and you will do yourself and your career a favour.

Figure 10.1 ends this chapter by showing a simplified example of a form often involved in the appraisal process.

JOB HOLDER'S NAME: DATE:

JOB TITLE:

ASSESSOR'S NAME:

ASSESSMENT OF KEY TASKS:

Key task:	Results achieved against performance standards	Assessment

What is your overall assessment of job holder's performance?

What are their strengths?

Their areas for improvement

Rating: Outstanding   ❏   Average   ❏
         Above average   ❏   Needs training and improvements   ❏
                                     Poor   ❏

Figure 10.1: Example Appraisal Form

What specific training and experience does the job holder need in the next 12 months?

1.

2.

3.

ACTION:
– arrange the next meeting;
– has the job changed since the last appraisal? If any of the Key Tasks or Performance Standards are inappropriate then redraft them on the Action Plan.

Comments by Assessor's Senior

Signed: Date:

Assessor's signature: Date

Job holder's comments

Signed: Date:

Figure 10.1: Example Appraisal Form (continued)

Onwards and Upwards

'It is a funny thing about life: if you refuse to accept anything but the best, you very often get it.'

W. Somerset Maugham

FEW PEOPLE spend their entire career with one employer, and some of those few who do are in large multinational entities where effectively they are a conglomeration of different companies. So you may well come to the point where changing jobs is the only way in which you see the possibility of continuing to develop your career. This book, as you know, is not presenting a blueprint for applying for new jobs, but there are some issues here that fit our brief and when moving jobs are things you should have in mind well in advance before taking any steps to do so.

Choose the right moment to go

Get the timing wrong and the funniest story will fall flat. Get the timing wrong in a career and the same can happen. You need to consider this from two angles. First, when you should initiate action to seek another appointment, and second when it is right to take advantage of an opportunity that presents itself.

In both cases, the thinking starts with a review of the prospects within your existing situation. If you have a plan (and if you did not before, then by this stage of reading through this book you should have) that is the place to start. Is it likely that a new position would better enable you to reach your objectives than continued progress where you are now? You have to balance the devil you know against something inherently less known, but, quite possibly, no more difficult to predict. For many people the temptation to stay put and not, as they see it, take a risk is very great. On the other hand, if the offer comes to you, that always feels flattering and maybe difficult to resist as you compare a current employer where your progress is slower than you would wish, with someone who is, perhaps enthusiastically, offering an immediate change and a jump in salary.

Several issues may form a part of the decision:

- *Predictability:* In some organizations formal career planning is well spelt out. You know with reasonable certainty the kind of progress that you are likely to make and you may have to balance this against something less predictable. Of course, the reverse may be the case – you have no idea what even the next year with your current employer will bring, and you have to put that alongside firm offers and changes from elsewhere.
- *Speed of progression:* This needs assessing separately from predictability. For example, my own move out of the publishing industry was based mostly on this factor. However well I might have done I was going to spend too long at the lower levels, not least of earnings, to suit my plan; offered something else attractive which jumped me forward, I took it. The downside of this could be that what you select produces immediate progress but then a halt; though I have no regrets.
- *Future opportunity:* One option may hold out better long-term prospects than another and such decisions should always look well ahead, so far as you are able to do so.
- *Current prospects:* These need objective consideration. It is easy to underrate the situation with a current employer when faced – blinded perhaps – with a new opportunity.

Then of course there is the job itself – the current one or another – and all that they entail or might entail. Go back to your objectives. Objectives are dynamic. You do not have to step out of education, form some plans and then never change them; least of all in a successful career where you may decide to become more and more ambitious. For example, being on the Board may not be among your aspirations early on. Then you do sufficiently well to see it as actually a real option, and a move to achieve it may be exactly what you should then be planning.

It is valid too to see a move as temporary. One of the clearest examples of this is those people who work for a while overseas, or with an international company, or both, to give themselves this particular kind of experience. Also a valid part of weighing up options is to consider future regrets if a possible course of action is *not* followed. Again in my own case, when I was setting up my own firm it was, for all sorts of reasons, what I wanted to do. At the same time there were also other options. Amongst everything else, the feeling that if I did not try being my own boss then I would regret it for evermore, ran high. This feeling was made stronger by the fact that it would probably have been more difficult to do it later than it was at the time (such an option is rarely easy, but, in my case, so far so good!). It is no good having a reasonable job but spending your life looking back and saying to yourself, 'If only I had . . .' You can never wind the clock back.

Finally, another measure may be useful. It is said that if you are not going forward it is time for a change. Everyone wants a job in which they continue to learn and develop. If a job has ceased to provide this and becomes merely repetitive, then it may be time to move on. If you have other options, either offered or sought out, consider them carefully and always remember there are three options: staying and progressing where you are; taking an offer that has arisen to go elsewhere; or going out to find someone who will make you another, better, offer. The latter could be harder work than taking something offered and there on a plate, but it could be the best bet in the long run.

Be well equipped to move

If you stay too long with one organization, you may be regarded as having limited experience (though what recruiters regard as 'too long' varies a good deal). Conversely, if you have a CV that shows a career record of ceaseless change you may come to be regarded as a 'job-hopper' and less attractive because of that. Certainly, it is quite possible that, whichever your circumstance, the time you spend with one employer lets your job-hunting skills atrophy. Career development of the sort discussed here includes positive action to prevent this happening. Several things can be done, among them the following.

Always keep your CV up to date. Most job hunting necessitates having an up-to-date statement of your background, qualifications and experience; even someone approaching you may want this, so will recruitment agencies and consultants. CVs quickly get out of date. It is not sufficient for them to say who you worked with and your job title, certainly for more recent jobs they should spend some of their limited space describing achievements and what you can do for someone else and how. So make notes, review the document regularly and update as necessary (word processors make this much easier than in the past).

Finally, I want to make an obvious statement: you need a well-constructed and well-written CV – it is a selling document and there can be no half measures. It is either good enough to play its part in getting you a new job or it is useless, just so much waste paper.

Incidentally the covering letter that goes with a CV is also vital. In both cases, despite all the detailed published advice about them, the prevailing standards are not so high that you cannot score points and differentiate yourself by producing a really good one. Remember too that, while you may keep a standard document on file, you may need to tailor it to each particular job application.

There are agencies, consultants and advisers who can help you prepare both (though vet them and choose carefully). There are also many good books on the subject, but given some thought it is surely something most people should be able to do themselves. A good CV must incorporate some of the current practice demanded by employers, but also needs to include elements that make it stand out in some way from the herd. It must be prepared carefully and then amended one by one to make them relevant to each and every different potential employer to whom you might send them.

Keep your interview skills up to date. This may be more difficult than editing or revising your CV, but anything you do infrequently tends to be more difficult than something you are able to practise. As a result, some would say it is worthwhile to apply for a job now and then, not because you intend to take it (or at least not on the evidence to hand), but just to give yourself interview practice.

I am conscious of the horror this will engender in any recruiter reading this; it is difficult enough to undertake a selection campaign without the picture being clouded by a host of people practising interview techniques, so I will add that this is very much not something to be overdone; but it is a thought. Another route to practise is on a course or in a tutorial with a consultant.

Review the press and keep in touch with agencies. You need to know what is the state of the market, who is hiring, what rates are being paid, and this too needs an active approach.

Take action to move thoroughly and well

Competition for jobs in most economies is often considerable. The points above about keeping up to date are part of the answer, but

once you are into the process every action must be executed carefully and well. This includes:

- reading job advertisements or other job descriptions carefully;
- writing (or adapting) covering letters to suit each different job
  and employer (and sometimes tailoring the CV too);
- filling in *all* of an application form and doing so clearly, thoroughly (I know much of the information is on the CV but
  recruiters find it easier to compare options presented in similar
  form, and so would you), and honestly – checks are made!
- preparing for interviews;
- being punctual;
- looking the part;
- taking the proceedings seriously;
- handling any follow-up efficiently (they may want additional
  information).

All this is really no more than common sense, but nothing that
might help make everything work that much better must be missed.
Try to put yourself in the position of the person attempting to fill a
job. It can be a thankless and difficult task, yet there is much hanging
on it, and the costs of getting it wrong are certainly high. They expect
you to be well turned out, they recognize that few recruitments result
in the appointment of anyone who turns out to be better than was
thought, though some do work out the other way round.

Make it easy for them to see they are dealing with a professional,
someone who is at some pains to help them make the right decision,
and your success rate is likely to be higher. This is very obviously a
key area, one of many details, and one where further reading is likely to be worthwhile.

Always leave on good terms

Perhaps a seemingly small and simple point, but one that can prove
invaluable later on; sometimes much later. No one's time in any
organization is entirely positive. You are unlikely to see eye-to-eye
with the boss or others over everything. There will be those who
always got right up your nose and others whose minor niggles characterized your every dealing with them. Then you leave and move
on. This is not the time to indulge yourself with righteous indigna-
tion, still less revenge – even a barbed remark in a resignation letter,

final report or memo may be remembered and quoted later out of context. Leave with good grace. Say something about the good things, of which there were presumably some if you have opted to stay there for a while, and aim not to make anyone even remotely like an enemy as you take your leave.

If you ask why – and the temptation for at least some throw-away jibe may be great – the reason is that you never know where your ex-colleagues (and ex-boss, for that matter) will end up. They may move on too. You may need a reference, or advice or information. This is a two-way street, and it may be worth indicating to people you may find useful in future that you hope to keep in touch, and that should they think you can help them in future they should not hesitate to say so. There may be contacts that need active maintenance, people with whom you begin to network, and these need adding to any reminder system you use.

Of course, none of these points should be taken as inferring that there are bound to be difficulties; there may be few or no problems as you move on. Nor does it imply that there will not be people with whom you will not easily and naturally keep up contact with on either a social or business basis, or both. That is as it should be. But during the run-up to a change, and certainly during the time the change is actually taking place, it is worth a little thought to smooth the path. Do not be like an old friend of mine who landed an excellent new job and moved on. I asked him later if he had left on good terms. 'Certainly', he said, 'it was all fine right up to the drinks in the office on the day I left. I drank a little too much and poured a beer over the MD's head!' You never know who will be useful in future, so never jeopardize a good relationship inadvertently, or for no good reason. Good contacts, and friendships, are too valuable to waste.

Do not underestimate the difficulty

Countries, economies and times vary but if you have to get another job – because your contract has expired, you have been made redundant or, in the worst case, you have been fired – do not ever underestimate the time and effort that may be involved in obtaining a new job; certainly the right new job. If the economy is strong, employment high and skilled and experienced people are in high demand, then there may well be little problem. If so – great. If not, or if luck is against you, then you need to take the appropriate action and do so wisely and fast. A prolonged period of unemployment does not look good on your record and after a while, rightly or wrongly, it gets more difficult for you to interest new employers. They may, understandably, view the gap as suspicious and view other candidates more favourably.

So, what does not underestimating what needs to be done mean? An earlier point was about all action taken needing to be done thoroughly and well. Here the point made concerns quantity. It is wisely said that searching for a job can be a full-time job in itself. There is a difference between being employed and beginning to look for something new with there being no pressure to move on quickly, and having to get another job before the lack of salary begins to seriously affect your lifestyle. After all, the time taken by the process itself can be considerable: an application goes out, even if successful it takes time to set up an interview, then perhaps a second one, with time in between as decisions are contemplated adding to what can quickly run into months rather than weeks. Make a real routine of the search, set specific time aside each day, and work through all the things to be done. These will include:

- checking all the media that carry job advertisements (newspapers, management journals, trade, professional and sectional magazines);
- contacting any appropriate recruitment agencies or consultants;
- research (some ads may look attractive, but you may not even be clear what business the organization is in; this and other details may be worth checking);
- writing and tailoring applications, and no doubt completing application forms;
- preparing for interviews you may obtain;
- writing to specific organizations even if they are not currently advertising;
- maintaining contact systematically with your network of people (or organizations) who might be able to help or might know someone else who might help;
- expanding your network of contacts – now is the time to attend all those association meetings and committees that were previously difficult to fit into your diary;
- keeping up-to-date in any way necessary with the technicalities of your business;
- doing any simple development you can fit in (even reading a business book may be useful).

You cannot really have too many applications out there prospecting for you, and it may be worth setting yourself some targets to make sure you do put enough 'bread on the waters'.

Certainly you should never stop or slow other activities because you have your sights optimistically on one particular job, even if you are sure things are going well. As was said, organizations can take time – weeks, sometimes months – to make a decision and if you do wait and slow down other activities, and then the answer is negative, the result is simply that you have lost time.

A systematic search will stand the best chance of getting you back into employment promptly and, after all, there is no harm in receiving more than one offer; you can always choose the best.

With 'a job for life' very largely a redundant phrase, progress may well ultimately involve moving from one organization to another or even to a different way of working. Nothing wrong with that. But, whatever the direction, progress is more certain if the route is travelled along with care.

Afterword

'There are no short cuts to any place worth going.'
Beverly Sills

THERE IS NO SINGLE career-boosting magic formula – what influences your success is the effect of many, many different things and the cumulative impact of them all. Even if you get most of the factors right, unforeseen circumstances may blow you off course and do so for no fault of your own, forcing you to redouble your efforts. So getting every detail right is well worthwhile.

There are other options to career development:

- *Buy the organization.* Nothing, as they say, beats ownership. This automatically puts you on top of the heap. Of course there are snags. They may not want to be bought. They may not be worth buying and there is the small matter of the necessary money. Again, while of course this happens, it does not really form a serious suggestion in the context of this book, at least not for many people; though in an age where buyouts is a word constantly in the press, perhaps it is for some.
- *Start your own business.* Now this may be a perfectly sensible career route and not, in fact, one that only makes sense when other possibilities have been exhausted. Small companies are a fast-developing part of many countries' economies, and are regularly an option for the final few years of a career. It is the route I have (finally) taken myself, so it deserves some sensible comment.

First, the advantages; drawing on a recent survey of why people set up in business, the reasons listed were as follows:

- To achieve greater independence.
- To make more money (and raise the ceiling).

- To change the nature of the work done.
- Dislike of big company culture.
- To have more free time.
- To work from home.

For many people, independence is more important than money. All the rest make sense (the last clearly only applies to a minority that this suits), and they are not mutually exclusive; all may play a part. It is a seductive mix and many are tempted. But, as with all seemingly good things there is always a 'But': there are other factors to consider, two in particular – first, you have to be prepared to take a risk. This is not something everybody can live with and if you are not content unless there is a regular salary cheque coming in then it may not be for you on this ground alone.

Second, you have to be able to run the business. Let me make that clearer: most of those who start up their own business have entrepreneurial skills and often specialized skills in one particular area. They are a talented engineer or designer perhaps, and intend to work in an area that plays to this strength. So far so good, but if you are in overall charge the buck stops with you – on everything. You may need other skills, broadly based to include management skills, accounting skills and sales skills, to name but three.

This may well be a real career option for some, but unless your skills are – across the board – up to the task, you should consider very carefully before you hand in your notice and erect a sign outside your new office. Remember the entrepreneur who insisted his lack of promotion and sales skills mattered not at all given the brilliant new business he was setting up. He started, and as he said, did no promotion or sales – right up to the moment he had to put a 'PREMISES FOR SALE' sign outside his ailing factory.

Finally, perhaps we should move on and end with one more thing . . . never become complacent; expect the unexpected.

What we have been reviewing here is a process that can be applied over many years, so the things that will happen, the twists and turns of fate that will occur during your career, will be many and varied. You can never anticipate them all, though you can expect they will be there. And you may well be able to take advantage of many of them, provided you have your wits about you.

Many things will occur; I can think of career changes in my own life influenced by factors as varied as the death of a colleague, a chance conversation, a company hitting economic difficulty, the discovery of abilities or possibilities not just which I did not know, but which I had discounted, and unexpected overseas travel.

Whatever stage you are at in your career, you will no doubt be able to look back on some things which have similarly already had an influence; and there will in all probability be many more to come. Be ready for them. Not specifically – you cannot know what is round the corner – but if you develop the habit of looking for opportunity in everything, then some of these random factors can be made to work for you.

Towards the future

However you decide to rank the most important factors in your life – home, family, partner, health – your job will rank high in the list: it takes up a very significant part of your life. If it interests you, this is important; if you enjoy it and find it fun, so much the better. If you can achieve all these and find something that meets whatever other list of priorities you put on it, factors as diverse as, for example, location and security, and at which you can achieve a satisfactory reward and recognition, you may be well pleased.

But, and this was said early on, it will not just happen. What is more, the statistics are not in your favour. Pyramid-shaped organizations, by their very nature, have more people in them at lower levels than higher ones. So career development needs working at. So too, of course, does finding a job. It has not been the intention here to review that complete process, but rather to review how exactly you can work at career development in a way that increases the chances of getting where you want more rapidly and more certainly than would otherwise be the case.

I have not, in writing this book, had any preconceived idea of success in mind, certainly not seeing being Chief Executive as the only or most desirable goal. The point is to set your own objectives and then take conscious action that will get you as close as possible to those goals, whatever they may be; though there are almost certainly greater dangers in aiming too low than in aiming high. Vision and ambition together are a powerful combination. Compare the personal situation with that of a company. It is said that many companies could make a success of being in the taxi business, but that only the one who defines their business more broadly as 'transportation' and backs it up with visionary implementation, will ever go to the moon! So too for careers; sights should therefore be set reasonably high.

To achieve what you want, and make career development work for you, there is regrettably no guaranteed magic formula. Of course, luck can and does play a part – so too can the old premise of making your own luck – but luck is not to be relied on, and just waiting for it to happen is simply not one of the options. You need to take positive action. More than that, you need to take regular, ongoing action. Career development can perhaps be well described as a campaign, one that continues as long as you work, for you can never rest on your laurels. Competition is ever present and opportunities will often not wait. If you take your eye off the ball as it were, even briefly, your career prospects can change in a moment. This can result in a step back or a step forward. So what does work? Which are the things that make the difference? Many work at it a little – and hope – but others seem to get it right, in some cases consistently right and succeed sometimes beyond even their wildest dreams.

What is necessary is an all-embracing attitude to the task. You need to see all the activities in which you are involved – and a selection of them have been reviewed here both to give attention to the priorities and to illustrate the range of different types of influence – in two parallel ways: in terms of how they work for you in the job you have and the tasks which that currently involves, and in terms also of what effect they may have on your career.

The effect you then achieve is cumulative, you build up a situation which progressively makes your career more likely to progress successfully. Some of the inputs are small, others may be more significant. Together, however, they are capable of adding up to something that can give you an edge that will get you where you want to be. And if everything you do works well, the overall effect can be very powerful.

However it works out, whatever position you end up in, perhaps two points are more important than any others. First, that at the end of the day you feel that any success you enjoy was something you made happen, and that you have not missed taking all reasonable steps (you do not want to spend your life looking back and saying 'If only . . .', hence the conscious and systematic approach I have advocated).

Second, that wherever it takes you, you enjoy the journey as much as possible. To sum up, I would like to quote the journalist and columnist Katherine Whitehorn who said: 'The best careers advice to give the young is: find out what you like doing and get someone to pay you for doing it.'

That sounds good at any age.

Finally, I will not wish you luck, after what was said earlier, but I certainly wish you well with your career, whatever it may be.

References

Certain topics touched on here, and that readers may want to explore further, link to the author's other books such as:

Agreed! Making Management Communication More Persuasive (Kogan Page).
How to be Better at Writing Reports and Proposals (Kogan Page).
Conducting Successful Negotiations (How to Books).
Making Meetings Work (IPD Training Extra).
First Things First (on time management) (Pitman Publishing).
Making Successful Presentations (Sheldon Business Books).

The following, mentioned in the text, may also be useful:

Managing Ideas for Profit (Simon Majaro, McGraw-Hill).
In Search of Excellence (T. J. Peters and R. H. Waterman).
How to Succeed in Psychometric Tests (David Cohen, Sheldon Press).

Some of the material on decision-making, and the ongoing development cycle, is adapted from a section of an earlier book (now out of print) *Running an Effective Sales Office*. This was written during my time with the Marketing Improvements Group, and I am grateful for allowing it to reflect some of the corporate thinking of that company.

Index